THE THREE PILLARS OF STOICISM

DEVELOP CHARACTER IN ACCORDANCE WITH
THE STOIC IDEAL THROUGH THE LIVES AND
TEACHINGS OF SENECA, EPICTETUS, AND
MARCUS AURELIUS

THINKNETIC

CONTENTS

GET 3 FREE BONUSES!

Free Bonus #1
Our Bestseller *Critical Thinking In A Nutshell*

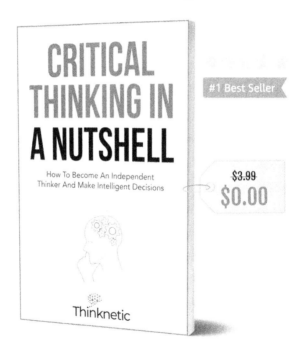

Did You Know That 93% Of CEOs Agree That This Skill Is More Important Than Your College Degree?

Here's just a fraction of what you'll discover inside:

- How to shortcut the famous Malcom Gladwell "10,000 Hours Rule" to become an expert critical thinker, fast
- What a WW2 pilot and the people of Romania can teach you about critical thinking - this is the KEY to not making huge mistakes
- Actionable, easy exercises to drill home every point covered in the novel. You won't "read and forget" this book

★ ★ ★ ★ ★

"This book is a good primer for the beginner and a good refresh for the expert who wants to bring more critical thinking into their problem-solving. Easy to read and understand, buy this book."

(Kevin on April 19, 2021)

"This book is unlike any other on Critical Thinking. The author puts an entirely new twist in critical thinking. Very easy to understand. Give it a read and see for yourself."

(Knowledge Seeker on April 16, 2021)

"The explanations are straight forward, sensible and usable with some interesting ideas about how this can be taught or learned."

(Dave Crisp on April 14, 2021)

Free Bonus #2
Thinking Cheat Sheet *Break Your Thinking Patterns*

Free Bonus #3
Thinking Guide *Flex Your Wisdom Muscle*

<u>A glimpse into what you'll discover inside:</u>

- If your thinking is flawed and what it takes to fix it (the solutions are included)
- Tried and true hacks to elevate your rationality and change your life for the better
- Enlightening principles to guide your thoughts and actions (gathered from the wisest men of all time)

Go to thinknetic.net to download for free!

(Or simply scan the code with your camera)

INTRODUCTION

During high school, many of us probably found world history difficult for one reason. It is difficult to memorize the names, dates, places, and events that we did not witness personally and, therefore, attach little meaning to. However, my classmates and I were lucky to have a history teacher who brought the past to life by focusing on the stories behind the names, dates, and places. By vividly describing how people lived, why they did certain things, and especially how their thoughts and actions were shaped by their environment, these people came to life. The past became, for us, a rich repository from which we draw insights, understanding, and inspiration.

The lessons of history prove useful when the demands of modern living take their toll on us. This is true not only for those who are struggling and failing but also for those who are succeeding. Those among us who strive to achieve perfection in our careers, businesses, or vocations are often rewarded with fortune, fame, or power. Along the journey, problems arise, time is too short, and things do not go according to plan. And even when we attain the height of success, we become the target of others' jealousy, ill intent, or malicious gossip that tarnish our reputation. Sometimes the same drive and ambition that sustains our efforts to succeed become the cause of our stress and unhappiness. Failure and success become one, and neither provides the happiness we seek.

Somewhere in the recesses of the human heart, we have the sense that the solution to our problems lies within ourselves. We have inner strength, but when we give way to worry and distress, we lose track of that ability to face our problems with calm and discernment. The confusion of the moment distracts us from thinking and deciding rationally. So how could we avoid the moment of noise and confusion? Would it not be wonderful if we could readily unlock that wellspring of wisdom that resides within us?

This book aims to help us do just that – renew ourselves with fresh insights from the past. We focus on the lives and teachings of the three most beloved Stoic philosophers in history – the paradoxical Seneca, Epictetus the slave, and Marcus Aurelius, the emperor. Chapter 1 lays down the beginnings of Stoicism. Then each philosopher is featured in chronological order every two chapters after that. Chapters 2 and 3 discuss Seneca, Chapters 4 and 5 deal with Epictetus, and Chapters 6 and 7 speak of Marcus Aurelius. The first chapter of each set is a brief biography of the philosopher. Two elements are highlighted here: the unique circumstances of his life that led to his philosophical development and the events in his life that demonstrate how he practiced his Stoicism. The next chapter presents a discussion of the themes most associated with his teachings, embodied in selections from his writings. Stories of relevant contemporary people and situations are selected to illustrate the themes, enabling the readers to link the past to the present better.

This book is designed to both inform and delight. The author, yours truly, nurtures a fondness for ancient history. I formally studied Roman philosophy in tandem with Roman law and its influence on contemporary legal theory. Personally, I hold a deep and abiding fascination for the Stoic philosophers and their teachings. I applied them in my various careers as a college professor, engineer, stockbroker, financial analyst, and writer. In dealing with my subordinates on the job, my students in class, and my children at home, I always sought to impart a sense of self-control, forethought, and deliberate conduct reflective of the wisdom I found in the ancient teachings.

This book is intended to be a companion to the thoughtful reader who wants to understand, appreciate, and live Stoicism. It seeks to convey the lessons of Seneca, Epictetus, and Marcus Aurelius in such a way that they become real to you, the reader, speaking to you in the context of your daily activities. Hopefully, as you move through these pages, you may be delighted, moved, and struck by flashes of inspiration, that in the end, you may find the Stoic philosopher that lies within you.

Are you ready to take a journey through the ages? Then let's begin.

Dianna Gene P. Aquino

1

STOICISM AT A GLANCE

> I conceived the bold and arduous project of arriving at moral perfection. I wished to live without committing any fault at any time; I would conquer all that either natural inclination, custom, or company might lead me into.[1]
>
> — BENJAMIN FRANKLIN

The son of a candlemaker and grandson of a blacksmith, he was born into poverty on January 17, 1706, as the fifteenth child of a brood of seventeen. He only had two years of schooling in his whole life. But he grew up with the resolve to live a life of virtue and moral rectitude. He always observed the Thirteen Virtues – temperance, silence, order, resolution, frugality, industry, sincerity, justice, moderation, cleanliness, tranquility, chastity, and humility. He taught himself through rigorous self-study and became a printer, scientist, inventor, musician, author, and statesman. He learned to speak French, Italian, Spanish, and Latin.[2] Moreover, Benjamin Franklin became a founding father of the greatest country in the world, the United States of America.

Franklin is an example of the vast possibilities that a life dedicated to attaining virtue may lead to, not only for oneself but also for others and humanity in general. Because of his strict adherence to a life of virtue and strict self-discipline, many have wondered whether he was an avowed Stoic or at least consciously and openly lived by the tenets of Stoicism. Franklin lived in the America of the 1700s. Stoicism began as a philosophy at the time of ancient Greece. Is there a connection between them? We will try to resolve this question at the end of this chapter. But first, let us get to know more about Stoicism.

Definition Of Stoicism

The Oxford English dictionary defined Stoicism as "An ancient Greek school of philosophy founded at Athens by Zeno of Citium." (Oxford Lexico) [3]. The philosophy centered on virtue as the highest good and knowledge as the source of virtue. Generally accepted as the four virtues of Stoicism are courage, temperance, justice, and wisdom. Wisdom resulted from living in harmony with divine Reason that governs nature. Pain, pleasure, and the changing circumstances of fortune are inconsequential to a virtuous life.

More than the dictionary definition, Stoicism is a living philosophy.[4] It goes beyond the simple description that appears to apply to so many other inanimate objects but an organic thing that grows, transforms, and bears fruit. According to the people who live by Stoic philosophy, these individuals fashion their lifestyles through considerations independent of their economic or social status. The true spirit of Stoicism is the result of millennia of philosophical development. Tracing this development from its earliest beginnings would provide a clearer perspective of its continued relevance into the future.

Pre-Stoic Background

The first seeds of all philosophy, Stoicism included, may be traced to Heraclitus (535-475 BCE). A nobleman of Ephesus, he is credited as being the first to articulate the idea of logos, a crucial Stoic concept that combines reason and judgment. Legend has it that he was born to ascend the throne but abdicated to pursue his study of philosophy instead. Among those who admired his teachings were Socrates, Plato, Aristotle, until Goethe, and even modern quantum physicists found relevance in his works.[5]

Unfortunately, Heraclitus' original writings were lost to the ages, and only fragments referencing him were found in others' writings. From these sources, historians credited Heraclitus as the originator of the concept of Logos as the rational divine intelligence. He is the father of cosmology, where an orderly universe fundamentally comprises fire as its basic element. He envisioned the world as a coherent system of opposites such that where a change creates an imbalance, a corresponding change occurs to restore the balance. Heraclitus taught that for people to be happy, they should live harmoniously according to the universal principle of Logos or Reason. It is this emphasis on Logos that forms the theoretical foundation from which Stoicism will emerge.[6]

The next philosopher noted after Heraclitus is Socrates (469-399 BCE), who taught about searching for wisdom leading to right conduct. The son of a stonemason and a midwife, Socrates was born of humble origins. However, according to early accounts, an early Oracle of Delphi indicated to him that there was no wiser man in Greece than himself. Socrates found this incredible, and in trying to prove (or disprove) it, he went about questioning the learned elite in Athens to find one who was wiser than him. The series of questions became tests of logic and led to discovering layers of beliefs about a topic.

Based on Socrates' teachings, Plato (428/427 – 348/347 BCE) founded the Academy. This was not a formal school or college but rather an informal gathering of intellectuals who engaged in philosophy, mathematics, astronomy, and other subjects of interest in their discourses. It was founded on the belief that knowledge resulted from inner reflection and external observation and could be passed onto others through instruction.[7]

At about the same time as Plato, another popular discipline of Socrates was Antisthenes (446-366 BCE), the commoner. He founded the Cynic school of philosophy, which taught a set of ideas that lead to a more thoughtful and ultimately happier life. These teachings were rooted in an awareness of the contradictions and injustices of society. Moral virtue leads to happiness, and that teaching could convey what makes life virtuous.[8]

The Academy And The Cynic Schools

The philosophical teachings of Heraclitus, Socrates, Plato, and Antisthenes were the foundations upon which early Stoicism found its roots. However, the founding of Stoicism itself as a school of thought can be directly traced to two philosophical schools, particularly the Academy and the Cynic schools. Zeno of Citium, who eventually founded Stoicism, was a student of both these philosophical schools, therefore to understand Stoicism, it is important to understand its connection to Plato's Academy and Antisthenes's Cynicism. The direct line of descent in philosophical teachings proceeded from Antisthenes to Diogenes to Crates and finally to Zeno.

Compared to his master Antisthenes, Diogenes preached and practiced a more ascetic lifestyle. For example, he lived in a discarded bathtub, slept in discarded buildings, and begged for his food.[9] Practitioners of this lifestyle forsook all materials possessions and were therefore called Cynics, which meant "dogs" in Greek.[10] Crates of Thebes, also known as the Good Genius, took over the school from Diogenes. Historical accounts say that he gave away his fortune to live an impoverished life in Athens' streets.[11] As the leader of the Cynic school, Crates became the direct teacher of Zeno. While Zeno was influenced by both the Academy and Cynicism, he eventually established his own philosophical school, Stoicism, which exists until today.

Zeno Of Citium (334-262 Bce)

The ancient Greek philosopher Zeno of Citium is acknowledged to be the founder of Stoicism. He was born a citizen of Citium, Cyprus, in the year 335 BC. His father, Mnascas, was a prosperous merchant whose ships plied the Mediterranean and Aegean routes. There is no account of Zeno's early life; what little was written about him began when he was thirty.

The Stoicism envisioned by Zeno is applied to everyday life, comprised of three areas of study: (1) ethics, the study of how we should live our lives; (2) physics, now known as the natural sciences, metaphysics, and theology; and (3) logic (logos), or the study of how to reason about the world. Physics and Logos are the areas of study that nurture Ethics. The interrelationship of the three *topoi* could be illustrated in this manner: Ethics are the fruits of the tree of Stoicism, Physics is the soil that provides nutrition to the tree, and Logos is the fence that defines the boundaries of the garden of Stoicism.[12]

Zeno's life as a philosopher began after he barely survived a shipwreck on a voyage between Phoenicia and Piraeus in Greece.[13] In some writings, Zeno's account of this shipwreck was taken figuratively to mean that Zeno's life was meaningless before coming to Athens.[14] From his shipwreck until the time of his death, Zeno lived in Athens. In his study of logic, he found the mental focus and discipline he lacked as a merchant. He devoted himself to his studies and to eventually practicing what he learned. Among his teachings, he argued that virtue, and not pleasure, constituted the only good and that the key principle of the universe is embodied in the natural law rather than "the random swerving of atoms."[15]

There are several other noteworthy early Stoic philosophers, including Chrysippus (279-206 BCE), Posidonius (135-151 BCE), Cicero (106-43 BCE), and Gaius Musonius Rufus (30-101 CE). Each of these famous philosophers carried forward the fundamental Stoic philosophy of Zeno of Citium. Of the four, scholars believe that Musonius most significantly contributed to the development of Stoicism.

Gaius Musonius Rufus (30-101 Ce)

Gaius Musonius Rufus is regarded as one of the four great Stoic philosophers of the Roman empire, with Seneca, Epictetus, and Marcus Aurelius. Musonius' teaching mirrors that of Zeno insofar as he commits to virtue, rather than pleasure, being the source of all good. Austere personal habits bring one closer to a life of virtue.

These habits include a simple vegetarian diet, minimal garments, footwear, denouncing an expensive lifestyle, and embracing a sturdy life. Unfortunately, none of Musonius' own writings have survived until today, if ever there were any. Others preserved his teachings in the form of 32 apothegms (concise sayings or maxims) and 21 long discourses. It is believed that Musonius conducted his lectures in Greek because most of the writings were in Greek, with just one, a testimonial by Aulus Gellius, written in Latin.[16]

Many of Musonius' teachings [17] were ahead of their time, and several of them reflect surprisingly contemporary thinking, not socially acceptable a little over a century ago. Musonius believed that women were entitled to receive the same philosophical education as men and supported it with the following arguments. First, the gods endowed women with the same power of reason as men. Second, women possess the same senses as men–i.e., sight, hearing, smell, touch, and taste, by which they can observe their environment. Third, both sexes share similar body parts–head, arms, torso, legs. Fourth, like men, women desire virtue and are naturally drawn to it, taking pleasure in nobility and justice and repulsion in their opposites. A woman, therefore, could manage an estate, supervise a household staff, and exercise self-control. She will become a good and like-minded life partner to her husband, and protector, teacher, and model to her children.

In many ways, Musonius's teachings shunned modern-day liberality and embraced conservative values. Consistent with Stoicism, Musonius opposed luxurious living. He associated the life of the rich with licentious sex, condemning all recreational sexual acts as contrary to a virtuous marital life, contrary to what is good. Adultery was unlawful and illegitimate, and homosexuality was against nature since the only legitimate sex acts aim to procreate within the marriage.

Musonius envisioned what makes a happy marriage. "[W]hen each spouse competes to surpass the other in giving complete care, the partnership is beautiful and admirable. But when a spouse considers only his or her own interests and neglect s the other's needs and concerns, their union is destroyed..."[18] Furthermore, "Marriage is the way for a person to create a family to provide the well-being of the city...[A]nyone who deprives people of marriage destroys the family, city, and the entire human race."[19]

The Three Pillars Of Stoicism

Musonius's teachings are consistent with the core of Stoicism, the school that the three pillars of Stoicism-Seneca, Epictetus, and Marcus Aurelius - expounded on. The following is a glimpse of the three, by way of introduction:

Lucius Annaeus Seneca (c. 4 BCE – 65 CE) was also known as Seneca the Younger.[20] Seneca's focus was on moral philosophy and ethical matters. He strongly emphasizes the shortness of life, endurance, and tranquility.[21] He is known for the following words of wisdom:

> Luck is what happens when preparation meets opportunity. [22]

> Begin at once to live, and count each separate day as a separate life. [23]

> If you want to escape the things that harass you, what you need is not to be in a different place but to be a different person. [24]

Epictetus (55 – 135 CE) [25] was born a slave but rose to become one of history's renowned philosophical sages. His body of work highlights freedom and the dichotomy of control–that is, an understanding of what is and is not within our control.[26] Epictetus wrote :

> Freedom is the only worthy goal in life. It is won by disregarding things that lie beyond our control.[27]

> Circumstances don't make the man; they only reveal him to himself. [28]

> People are not disturbed by things but by the views they take of them. [29]

Finally, Marcus Aurelius (121 – 180 CE) [30], Emperor of Rome. He typically emphasized that a virtuous life is one lived according to nature, which is a part of the Whole. Right exists in being consistent with the universe; wrong takes place by going against it. [31] He is known for the following nuggets of wisdom.

> The happiness of your life depends upon the quality of your thoughts. [32]

> Do every act of your life as though it were the very last act of your life. [33]

> Live out your life in truth and justice, tolerant of those who are neither true nor just. [34]

The following chapters will discuss more on these men and their teachings. For now, let us test our wits and understanding with the following exercise from Seneca, Epictetus, and Marcus Aurelius.

Action Steps

A distinct advantage to students of Stoic principles is their ready applicability to daily living. Enthusiasts devise many exercises in the Stoic tradition that are easy to do and provide fresh perspectives about themselves. The Daily Stoic [35] provides us with some useful exercises to assimilate the Stoic viewpoint. Here are five that you may find challenging and quite beneficial.

(1) <u>The Dichotomy of Control</u> – One of the more important Stoic lessons is to discern those matters that are within our control and those that are beyond it. Let's say an unfavorable event takes place, such as being late for an important appointment or not receiving the hoped-for promotion. The typical reaction is anger at oneself or another person. Assume a moment of quiet and analyze: "Is this something that was within my control or entirely out of my control? If it was, what can I do the next time when something like this happens to avoid the same outcome?" On the other hand, if it is beyond your control, no amount of cursing at the traffic or one's employer can change the outcome. Learn to accept things beyond your control with calm and resolve.

(2) <u>Journaling</u> – A common practice among the three philosophers involves writing down their thoughts about life and the day's events. These musings comprise a self-examination of one's deeds and utterances during the day – some call this an examination of conscience. This is something you can do to gain insight into yourself, your motivations, and your thoughts. Journaling at the end of the day is more fruitful if you hide or ignore nothing from yourself. You will gain a clearer perspective of yourself and how you may achieve greater peace and happiness in your life. And, you will get to sleep more soundly, having made peace with yourself!

(3) <u>Practice Misfortune</u> – This appears like a strange exercise. It involves adopting practices that you would do during times of misfortune, even if you are in the midst

of the most fortunate moments in your life! This means that even if you might be wealthy, you should practice living a life of poverty. This is not as far-fetched as it sounds. In 2009, the UK's Prince William spent one night sleeping on London's streets, emulating the life of the homeless.[36] Rather than just trying to imagine the situation, the actual experience is the key to this exercise. The purpose is to overcome your fear of the unknown consequences of misfortune by living through the experience and conquering the fear.

(4) <u>Turn the Obstacle Upside Down</u> – Also called training one's perceptions, this exercise involves turning something bad into a source of good. People say that the Chinese word for crisis refers to a juncture where "danger" and "opportunity" meet, a turning point. This approximates how a Stoic looks at life. There is no good or bad, only the perception of it. You may have lost the promotion, but someone else had the good fortune to receive it. There is some good in everything bad.

(5) <u>Take the View from Above</u> – This is not new to many of us; it involves taking the bird's eye view. The practice is also called "looking at the big picture." It involves looking outside ourselves, assuming ourselves to be "small" compared to humanity's broader view. For example, a garden party you may have planned towards the end of a long, hot summer may be ruined by an unexpected heavy fall of rain. Your first tendency is to curse the misfortune that rain should fall after three months of clear skies. However, taking the big picture may reveal that the rain is

a blessing for the farmlands that suffered from the drought or communities lacking water supply. You then realize that your personal misfortune is small compared to the larger good.

Moving On

After learning about Stoicism, is it possible to decide whether Benjamin Franklin was a Stoic or not? After a broad search, there does not appear to be any outright admission, written or otherwise, that Franklin identifies as a Stoic. However, there is sufficient evidence to say that he practiced the tenets of Stoicism. His Plan for Attaining Moral Perfection appears to be inspired by this ancient philosophy. [37]

The time-tested principles and practices of the Stoics that helped to build the nation remain relevant even after more than two thousand years ago. Three men made this possible. In the next chapter, we learn about the first of them, Seneca the Younger.

Chapter Summary

•Stoicism is a living philosophy centered on virtue as the highest good and knowledge as the source of virtue.

•There are four Stoic virtues: courage, temperance, justice, and wisdom.

•The ancient philosophers who contributed to the beginnings of Stoicism are Heraclitus, Socrates, Plato, and Antisthenes.

•Zeno of Citium is the father of Stoicism. His teachings were handed down through the generations through Chrysippus, Posidonius, Cicero, and Musonius.

•Musonius is the first of the four pillars of Stoicism. His teachings included rejecting the luxurious life and embracing a life of poverty. He believed women deserve the same education as men, and the goal of marriage was procreation.

•The three other pillars of Stoicism are Seneca, Epictetus, and Marcus Aurelius.

2

SENECA THE YOUNGER – THE MOST CONTROVERSIAL STOIC

> Throw me to the wolves and I will return leading the pack.[1]

— SENECA

Here's a challenge: Is the foregoing statement that of a Stoic philosopher? According to the Daily Stoic [2], the idea that "humility kills dangerous pride is at the core of Stoic philosophy." Well, that statement does not sound humble at all. Some would say it sounds rather "badass" if we were to quote the younger generation (the older generation would say "gung-ho"). But it is glowingly attributed to Seneca the Younger, the first of the three Stoic philosophers whom we shall get to know in this book.

Much like this saying, the life of Seneca, for a Stoic philosopher, is one fraught with paradoxes and contradictions. He grew up in a provincial setting and, during his lifetime, was subjected to disgrace and exile. Still, in his middle age, he was considered as one of Rome's most powerful personalities, particularly when he reached the pinnacle of his worldly success as emperor Nero's most trusted adviser. Despite his ascent, he increasingly felt alienated, imprisoned, and fearful of the position he occupied. He implored the emperor to be set free and allowed to retire, returning some of the wealth that the emperor had given him. In 64 CE, he withdrew from Nero's court, but by then, Seneca had already come under suspicion of conspiracy against the empire, which was the emperor's final judgment upon him.

Seneca's Early Life

Lucius Annaeus Seneca (c. 4 BCE – 65 CE) was called "the Younger" to distinguish him from his father, Lucius Annaeus Seneca. Accounts of his birth set it at somewhere between 4-1 BCE, in Corduba located in the Roman province of Baetica in Hispania, southern Spain, far removed from the power of metropolitan Rome.

In 5 CE, his maternal aunt brought him to Rome to be raised and educated in rhetoric and philosophy. Rhetoric, which is the art of persuasive writing and speaking, was considered a skill that orators and other learned men needed to master during ancient times. Philosophy is, of course, the study of wisdom and knowledge, of the fundamental nature of the world, and the relationship of people to the world and each other.

Seneca was a sickly youth, suffering from asthma and other illnesses. At about 20 CE, Seneca, who was in poor health for most of his life, went to Egypt for a long stay with his maternal aunt and uncle to improve his health.

Philosophical Training

When he arrived in Rome, Seneca first undertook the study of rhetoric. Later on, Seneca undertook the study of philosophy under his tutelage of his beloved mentors, Attalus the Stoic and Sotion the Sextian.

Attalus The Stoic

Seneca the Elder wrote in the Suasoriae (2.12): "Attalus the Stoic, who was banished thanks to the machinations of Sejanus, was a man of great eloquence, far more subtle and at the same time the most articulate of the philosophers seen in your generation" [3] (i.e., the time of his sons).

Seneca the Younger described in warm and somewhat nostalgic terms the days he undertook his formal study in the school of Attalus (Ep 108.3). Seneca recalled how Attalus taught an interesting form of self-restrained intellectual askesis, a rigorous form of self-discipline. Seneca was inspired by his teacher, describing how he was the first to arrive and last to leave and requesting his teacher to take up topics for discussion even while they were on walks together. Seneca saw Attalus as the kind of mentor who made himself available to students and took the extra effort to go out of his way to meet with them. Often, Seneca would refer to his teacher as Attalus noster ("our Attalus"); he was admired for his wisdom and exerted a strong and early influence on the young Seneca.

One area that Attalus had a strong interest in and which he passed onto his student Seneca was the Etruscan art of divination by sky signs, e.g., thunder and lightning (Natural Questions, 2.48.2, 2.50.1). This branch of physics is closely related to theology and ethics. Still, this particular combination of ethical and philosophical interests with physics appears to be a specific legacy that Attalus passed onto Seneca. [4]

Sotion And Papirius Fabianus From The School Of The Sextii

The school of the Sextii was a philosophical school in the Hellenistic {Classical Greek} sense dedicated to the pursuit of happiness. It defined itself as a philosophical-medical school that combined Pythagorean, Platonic, Cynic, and Stoic elements.[5] Sotion and Papirius Fabianus were both teachers of Seneca during his instruction under that school.

From Sotion (Ep. 49.2), Seneca acquired his admiration for Pythagoreanism, the teachings of Pythagoras best known for its mathematical discoveries and the relationship between music and mathematics (e.g., the Pythagorean theorem). Sotion also convinced Seneca in his early adulthood to become a vegetarian, a practice he adopted for at least a year. He eventually gave up the practice at his father's urging because it was associated with "some foreign rites."[6] Sotion thought of vegetarianism as part of the theory of the soul's migration. Seneca quoted Sotion's perspective as follows:

> You do not believe that souls are assigned, first to one body and then to another, and that our so-called death is merely a change of abode? You do not believe that in cattle, or in wild beasts, or in creatures of the deep, the soul of him who was once a man may linger? You do not believe that nothing on this earth is annihilated, but only changes its haunts? And that animals also have cycles of progress and an orbit for their souls, no less than the heavenly bodies, which revolve in fixed circuits? Great men have put faith in this idea; therefore, while holding to your own view, keep the whole question in abeyance in your mind. If the theory is true, it is a mark of purity to refrain from eating flesh; if it be false, it is economy. And what harm does it do to you to give such credence? I am merely depriving you of food which sustains lions and vultures.[7]

The other teacher in the school of the Sextii who significantly influenced Seneca's life is Papirius Fabianus, who is said to be highly respected by both Senecas, the Elder, and the Younger. The Younger recorded that Papirius' writings of note were on Physics.[8] He was also reputed to have been quite knowledgeable and experienced in matters of nature.

Adult Life And Occupation

By c.31, Seneca returned to Rome after his uncle died on the way back from Egypt. Upon his return to Rome, Seneca campaigned for his first magistracy. During this period, he gained a reputation as a skilled orator and eventually became a quaestor. A quaestor (literally "the man who asks questions") is one of the lowest ranking magistrates from the early Republic until the Roman Empire.[9]

The year c.37 marked the death of the emperor Tiberius and the accession of Caligula (c.37-41 CE). The year also marks the birth of Nero, son of Gnaeus Domitius Ahenobarbus, and Agrippina the Younger. As emperor of Rome, Nero will someday play an important part in the life of Seneca the Younger.

One year after Caligula became emperor, Seneca wrote De Consolatione ad Marciam (On Consolation to Marcia). The Consolations are letters written by Seneca in the Consolatio tradition, a literary genre encompassing essays, poems, speeches, and personal letters. Seneca wrote his consolations as essays, the Consolation to Marcia was written before his exile. In contrast, the other two famous consolations, the Consolation to Polybius and the Consolation to Helvia, were written during his exile. The Consolation to Marcia was intended to console her on the death of her son Metilius. Between c.37-41, Seneca wrote De Providentia (On Providence). This is described by some as a short essay, by others as a book, divided into six sections that discuss how the Stoic concept of Providence may be reconciled with the manifestation of evils in the world.[10] Briefly, the Stoic concept of Providence is that everything that happens has a divine cause and purpose and, therefore, cannot be evil. The next chapter will discuss Seneca's teachings more deeply.

Around the year c.38-39, Seneca the Elder died. It was also around this time when conflict arose between Caligula and Seneca the Younger. However, Seneca was spared execution due to his bad health (i.e., it was thought that his illness would shorten his life). Caligula is generally known to be unstable, and the severe conflict between him and Seneca was attributed possibly to Caligula's jealousy of Seneca's oratorical gift for which he was renowned.[11]

It was about c.40 when Seneca entered his first marriage, and his son was born, although the child died before his first year was over. He also began to build up his connections in court and struck up a friendship with Agrippina and Caligula's younger sister, Julia Livilla. These connections became quite providential because Agrippina eventually became Seneca's patron and staunch supporter. His friendship with Julia Livilla was also consequential but unfortunate since it was with her that Seneca was implicated in an adulterous affair that caused his exile.

Seneca's Exile

In January 41, the 38-year-old Caligula was assassinated by Cassius Chaerea, the tribune of the Praetorian Guard, and others who collaborated with him. Caligula's wife and daughter were also put to death, leaving his uncle Claudius (41-54 CE) to succeed as emperor.[12] During this year, Messalina, Seneca's wife, asked her husband to be banished to Corsica on a charge of adultery with Julia Livilla.

During his exile, Seneca focused on his philosophical studies and wrote several treatises. At about c. 43 or 44, Seneca wrote De Consolatione ad Polybium (On Consolation to Polybius). Polybius was the Literary Secretary of Emperor Claudius, and Seneca wrote the letter to console him in his brother's death. This letter is important because it depicts Seneca's life in exile. It is also definitive of his philosophy towards death, particularly on its inescapable reality.

During c. 46-48, Seneca wrote De Consolatione ad Helviam Matrem (On Consolation to Helvia), dedicated to his mother. Seneca sought to console his mother on his exile to Corsica. In this letter, Seneca employed the rhetorical devices of the Consolatio Tradition while simultaneously expressing his Stoic philosophy. In the Consolation to Helvia, Seneca plays the role of both the consoler and the cause of the pain inflicted, and this intention is acknowledged in the essay.

Another essay that Seneca began to write during his exile was De Brevitate Vitae (On the Shortness of Life). He began writing the essay in c. 48 and continued it until c.55, after his exile ended. Seneca addressed this letter to his father-in-law, Paulinus. The essay discusses several Stoic principles dealing with time and how people waste it in trivial pursuits. Seneca did not limit his writings to essays. While in exile, during the period c. 42-49, Seneca wrote the first two books of De Ira (On Anger) and addressed this to Lucius Annaeus Novatus, his elder brother. "On Anger" is consistent with the other writings of Seneca that aim to provide a guide for people to live a virtuous life free from vices that typically enslave them. Seneca saw anger as fundamentally wicked or evil. It is not something for people to control but rather to destroy, and Seneca provides advice about eliminating anger.

Seneca's exile ended in c. 49 when he won a recall from exile largely through the intervention of Agrippina, mother of Nero. Agrippina then hired Seneca to be the tutor of the rhetoric of the then twelve-year-old Prince Nero.

In the early hours of October 13 of 54 CE, Claudius, emperor of Rome, died after ingesting poisonous mushrooms. According to historians, Claudius was murdered, and consensus has that Agrippina, his wife, may have arranged it so that Nero, adopted by Claudius when he married Agrippina, may succeed before Britannicus, Claudius' natural son, could gain power. Nero's ascension enjoyed the support of the military and Burrus, the leader of the Guard. Nero was a popular favorite, being in direct lineage with Germanicus and the legendary Augustus, the first Roman emperor.

Nero was seventeen when he became emperor, making him the youngest emperor to date. Seneca, then Nero's tutor, also composed his speeches on at least three occasions: one speech for Nero's accession, a funeral speech for Claudius, and a speech addressed to the Senate under the new reign. After that, Emperor Nero appointed Seneca and Burrus as his advisors. In the year 56 CE, Seneca attained consulship, the highest position of political power in Rome. During Nero's early reign, Seneca and Burrus managed the affairs of the empire well, in the course of which they worked as a powerful tandem that drew the envy of others.

On March 23, 59 CE, Nero murdered his mother, Agrippina, with the acquiescence of Burrus. Agrippina's death was a blow to Seneca because she stood as his patron. Despite his assistance in Agrippina's murder, Burrus gradually lost favor over Nero. He died in 62 CE due to throat cancer, although it is speculated that Nero ordered that poison be administered to the dying Burrus.[13] Although Burrus was replaced, Seneca was not on good terms with Nero's praetorian prefects. He felt he was exposed, and his influence over Nero gradually waned. His enemies in the Senate felt Seneca's power slipping and began whispering accusations to gradually weaken his credibility, more common of which was his growing arrogance because of his wealth and eloquence. Probably the most damaging of these was the accusation that Seneca ridiculed Nero's chariot racing and his singing voice, although evidence was lacking.[14]

In the next two years, Seneca and other Roman financiers called in loans advanced to Britain (then a Roman province). Back then, Boudicca, the British Queen, led a revolt against Roman rule but failed in the attempt.[15] This matter will sometime in the future be used by historians through the ages as a posthumous accusation against the memory of Seneca (discussed in the next section).

Ever since Burrus' replacements, Tigellinus and Rufus, took over, Seneca felt his sway over Nero gradually abating. This erosion of his influence over the young emperor became most evident when Seneca failed to convince him not to execute his first wife, Octavia, or marry his mistress, Sabina. He, therefore, decided that, at age 65, he should retire while he still could. Nero accepted his offer of retirement.

Controversies Surrounding Seneca

History is not short on accounts concerning the inconsistencies between Seneca's actions and his words, mainly that while he extolled the Stoic life of poverty, he himself was leading a life of wealth and power, his so-called "monetary hypocrisy." [16] Many of these accusations appear to be conjectures and hypotheses, "baffling generalities, without specific references to the philosopher's writings." [17] While people derided Seneca because he possessed exorbitant wealth while he preached the virtues of leading an impoverished life, his detractors acknowledged that he had acquired his wealth honorably. [18]

There are several specific and public accusations leveled by a Roman Senator, Publius Suillius Rufus, against Seneca. According to the accounts by Tacitus and Cassius Dio, Suillius charged that:

(1) Seneca spent his time in idle studies in the company of inexperienced juveniles, and that he envied those who served the public and the larger good, such as Suillius;

(2) While he, Suillius, was nobly serving Germanicus as quaestor during the reign of Claudius, Seneca was seducing Julia, the daughter of Germanicus;

(3) Suillius' acceptance of a humble fee from a grateful client could not possibly equal Seneca's defilement of an imperial princess; and

(4) Within a mere four years, Seneca could not have amassed 300,000,000 sesterces (close to a billion US dollars following the gold standard) even with his philosophical and intellectual genius. But this he did, and he also lent money to Italy and the provinces at exorbitant

interest, and that his wealth was why many testaments were drawn in his favor. [19]

Tacitus notes that Suillius was highly prejudiced because Seneca had at one time successfully prosecuted him for corruption, for which half of his estate was confiscated and himself exiled.[20] Unfortunately, the accusations against Seneca were seeds that eventually took hold and tarnished Seneca's reputation at court and contributed to the events that led to his suicide. Even more than a hundred years after his death, these accusations were further embellished by the likes of Dio Cassius or his epitomizer Xiphilinus in 200 CE. These exaggerations included the following:

(1) Seneca not only seduced Germanicus' daughter, Julia, but he also flagrantly seduced young boys and was an adulterer with Nero's mother;

(2) Beyond acquiring the 300,000,000 sesterces, he also acquired 500 citrus-wood tables, each of which is mounted upon ivory legs, and upon which he served banquets; and

(3) Seneca's usury drained the provinces; moreover, it incited a rebellion throughout Britain. He forced the islanders to loan 40,000,000 sesterces from him against their will, then suddenly and to their detriment recalled his loan in its entirety. [21]

Through the final accusation above, Seneca's detractors conveniently exploited the revolt against Rome led by the British queen, Boudicca, mentioned in the preceding section. There is no evidence that the revolt, unfortunate as it was, could be attributed to Seneca's actions as a Roman official.

Seneca's Death

Lucius Annaeus Seneca died in 65 CE, and if anyone doubted that Seneca was a Stoic, the manner of his death proved it. A detailed account was written by the historian Tacitus one generation after Seneca died. The account was extremely vivid and intense: Seneca was forced to commit suicide to be involved in the Pisonian Conspiracy to assassinate emperor Nero.[22] He died with his friends by his side and in the company of his wife, who was willing to kill herself together with him.

When Seneca committed suicide, he was approximately 70 years old. He had a skinny physique as his regular diet consisted only of fruit and bread. Although he regularly exercised and kept himself physically active, he suffered from chronic bronchitis and asthma throughout his life, which contributed to his weakness in his old age.

His manner of suicide was not so easy, as several attempts had proved ineffectual. He first tried to cut his wrist, but when this proved insufficient to bring about his death, he drank the typical dose of hemlock. Eventually, he killed himself when he submerged himself in a hot bath and suffocated in the steam.[23] Tacitus observed that Seneca tried to model his death according to Socrates, who, after spending his last hours discussing philosophy with his close friends and students, died from drinking the poisoned hemlock. Tacitus appeared to imply that Seneca's self-centered approach in carrying out his own death diminished him in stature from Socrates, whom he sought to emulate.[24]

Seneca echoed Socrates in his claim that tota vita discendum est mori–"a wise man spends his whole life learning how to die."[25] Yet it is a paradox, one of many in Seneca's lifetime, that he died for reasons far removed from his philosophy. Seneca was closely involved in the politics and intrigues that pervaded Nero's court since he once served as the emperor's tutor, adviser, and speechwriter. Nero may have wanted Seneca eliminated because he probably suspected his former teacher of plotting against his life. Seneca's death revolved around issues that were entirely political and, therefore, inconsequential to his philosophy.

Seneca's death was far from the ideal Stoic death. Stoic philosophy asserts that the wise person leads a tranquil, happy, and free life. These conditions hold at all times for a true Stoic, even at the moment of death. However, Seneca's death was anything but these. His suicide attempts were a hit-and-miss affair. Although his wife planned to join him, she was saved by soldiers and eventually outlived her husband. And while the ideal Stoic philosopher leaves only his teachings as his legacy and little material value, Seneca had sufficient money and wealth to bequeath to his friends in his will in gratitude for the "services" they had rendered him. His critics felt that Seneca did not fit the image of a Stoic philosopher because he had the substantial wealth to give away in a will. He was concerned with how people will perceive him and his reputation after he has passed.[26]

Action Steps

In Chapter 1, we introduced Seneca by attributing to him the following quotes:

> Luck is what happens when preparation meets opportunity. [27]

> Begin at once to live, and count each separate day as a separate life. [28]

> If you really want to escape the things that harass you, what you need is not to be in a different place but to be a different person. [29]

Each of these quotes conveys meanings that are readily applicable in our daily lives. Choose one of them that speaks directly to you and, following the Stoic's practice of contemplation and journaling, write down the particular experiences in your life where this saying is particularly meaningful. Alternatively, you could look forward to your life and write about how you think this saying could be useful in improving your life as you plan for the future. Then keep this journal entry and look it up again one year from now. How have your thoughts and feelings changed during the time that has elapsed?

Moving On

Let's briefly revisit the opening saying attributed to Seneca: "Throw me to the wolves, and I will return leading the pack." A quick online scan shows that this is one of the most popular sayings attributed to Seneca, with one inspirational leadership website using it as a change motto.[30] People who read it think of aggression, impulsiveness, and blind courage. But after a reading of the life of Seneca, if indeed this statement is his, then it was certainly not meant to be brash and aggressive. Rather, it signifies conquering one's detractors with reason and example so that he may lead them to a better life. The next chapter will provide a fascinating look into Seneca's far-reaching insights.

Chapter Summary

•Seneca was born into a privileged life with wealth and luxury; nevertheless, he led a Stoic life.

•Among his teachers were the stalwarts of Stoicism, including Attalus, Sotion, and Papirius Fabianus.

•Seneca became the target of accusations that led him to exile, during which time he wrote some of his most notable literary works.

•Post-exile, Seneca became the tutor, adviser, and scriptwriter of the emperor Nero and served as an official of Rome.

•When his influence over Nero waned, Seneca retired but was eventually unfairly implicated in an attempt on the emperor's life.

•Seneca was forced to commit suicide and remained as controversial after death as he was during his life.

3

SENECA'S ESSAYS AND LETTERS THAT ARE GROUNDED ON STOICISM

> Cling tooth and nail to the following rule: Not to give in to adversity, never to trust prosperity, and always to take full note of fortune's habit of behaving just as she pleases, treating her as if she were actually going to do everything it is in her power to do. Whatever you have been expecting for some time comes as less of a shock.[1]
>
> — SENECA, LETTER 78, MORAL LETTERS TO LUCILLIUS

How wonderful it would be to win the lottery! I'm certain many of us would be ecstatic to win the multi-million-dollar first prize or even just a fraction of it, thinking that it would be the solution to all our problems! When Jack Whittaker won the largest jackpot awarded to a single Powerball ticket on Christmas day 2002, he doubtless felt that the lump sum of more than $113 million was the best Christmas gift ever.[2] Born in poverty, he worked his way up to own a small contracting company in West Virginia. He knew the value of a buck, and he did much good with his winnings, donating money for the Church and setting up charitable foundations. He also gifted a new house, a new car, and a good amount of cash to the woman who sold him the ticket.

But Jack's win was broadcast all over the state, and soon friends and strangers alike began writing to him for money. He lost no less than $600,000 in cash stolen from his car. He was hit with frivolous lawsuits from people who wanted their share of his money. He began drinking and paying for prostitutes. It was not long before he was unjustly implicated in the death of his granddaughter Brandi's boyfriend. Soon after, Brandi also died under suspicious circumstances, and after that, her mother. Whittaker's wife divorced him. He lost his family and his money. "I think if you have something, there's always someone that wants it," he later said. "I wish I'd torn that ticket up."

In Jack Whittaker's case, "fortune's habit of behaving just as she pleases" was evident in the way fortune appeared to smile on Jack one day and entirely deprive him of all that was valuable to him the next. Fortune is fickle, a fact that escapes us all. Jack's initial mistake is that he trusted in the permanence of his windfall prosperity. Then, overcome by adversity, he gave in to drinking and vice.

Certainly, Jack did not expect friends, clients, and even strangers to turn against him and take advantage of him. Most of all, he did not expect to lose the people he loved most, his family.

But Seneca knew. Almost two millennia ago, he understood how fortune could make a game of adversity and prosperity: "Not to give in to adversity, never to trust prosperity, and always to take full note of fortune's habit of behaving." The admonition to cling to this rule with all the power we have. We should be wary not to indulge too much when times are good and not fall prey to the despair of ill-fortune. To be aware of the extremes in life so as not to be caught unawares – that is Seneca's lesson.

General Thoughts About Seneca's Writings

Seneca had a vast pool of literary works, among which are literary speeches, private letters, poetry, works on India and Egypt, an early study of earthquakes, a treatise on marriage, and a book about his father, but more than half of these have been lost through the ages. Very little has survived about his early childhood and youth, and what has survived about him were largely written by others who were witness to his public life in the court of Nero. [3]

Seneca's writings that are still in existence remain voluminous, much more than other ancient authors. Tragedies, essays on various topics, philosophical letters, political satire, and a broad discussion on scientific matters (the Natural Questions) have survived him and provide us with a present-day insight into his philosophy. His literary works were focused on what makes life successful, delving into the contrasts between conflicting models of what ought to be a successful or good life.

The work that has survived about him also presents some problems for scholars of his life and work. According to Wilson [4], Seneca goes against the grain when it comes to his writing style because, unlike other early writers, he often used the first person and described in detail much of daily life during his time. But his works appear to have an indirect and complicated relationship with his life. Unlike the letters of Cicero to his friend Atticus that are highly biographical, some people feel that Seneca's works appear artificial and "carefully constructed works of performance, even the most apparently personal,"[5] such as the letter Seneca wrote his mother (Consolation to Helvia) while he was in exile. Rather than relate to her, his own mother, about his deepest sentiments and experiences in Corsica, Seneca's accounts appear to be mirroring the writings of Ovid, another famous Roman writer, concerning his (Ovid's) own exile.[6]

What is the relationship of reason to impulse, according to Stoicism? Some conceive reason as the guide and the impulse to the motive force, but this is not according to Seneca's belief that the impulse is identified with passion. The belief would elevate passion to the same level as the reason for the two to be equally vital for action. Passion, in the view of the Stoics, is equated with "an excessive impulse."[7] According to Stoic principles, for Seneca, reason is sufficient without anything else to supplement it.

Much of Seneca's voluminous writings that have survived to this day consist of wise sayings that we may directly relate to everyday life. He has written on practically every theme we encounter in our lifetime.

On Self-Esteem: Self-Worth Is Not Measured By Wealth Or Material Success

Seneca has been criticized through the centuries, from his contemporaries to the present day, for advocating the virtues of a frugal life while he possessed wealth and political power. But here's the rub – despite the loud protestations of detractors, Seneca has not been known to indulge in a luxurious lifestyle or misuse his political clout despite his wealth and position. Enemies leveled accusations against him, did so without evidence. The final analysis after two millennia points to the fact that Seneca, even though he was rich and powerful, did not allow his wealth and power to define his lifestyle. Seneca believed that a person's self-worth lies in the degree to which he leads a virtuous life.

 For the wise man does not consider himself unworthy of any gifts from Fortune's hands: he does not love wealth, but he would rather have it; he does not admit it into his heart but into his home; and what wealth is his he does not reject but keeps, wishing it to supply greater scope for him to practice his virtue.[8]

— SENECA, LETTER 92, MORAL LETTERS TO LUCILLIUS.

There are people like Seneca even today. Howard G. Buffett, the son of investment tycoon Warren Buffett, is worth at least the $2 billion his foundation received from his father, whose net worth is estimated at more than $65 billion. Yet, Howard has been an active worker his whole life, as a businessman, photographer, farmer, politician, sheriff, author, conservationist, and philanthropist. While Howard and his siblings were born to wealth, they had little financial support from their father growing up. Their parents taught them the value of work and thrift, creating value for humanity rather than squandering it.[9] Howard attributed his well-grounded perspective to his father, whose intention was to leave his children "enough money so that they would feel they could do anything, but not so much that they could do nothing."[10] It was as if Seneca had in mind the wisdom of the Buffetts when he wrote: "For the wise man regards wealth as a slave, the fool as a master."[11]

On Self-Awareness: Know Your Flaws And Never Allow Your Ego To Rule You

We agree with those who call us best and wisest, although we know they often utter many falsehoods: we indulge ourselves so greatly that we want to be praised for a virtue which is the opposite of our behavior. A man hears himself called 'most merciful' while he is inflicting torture. So it follows that we don't want to change because we believe we are already excellent.[12]

— SENECA, SELECTED LETTERS

Lance Armstrong was at the center of the sporting world's adulation when he won the Tour de France seven times in a row and retired at 33. There was much to be admired about this young man. At 25, he was diagnosed with third-stage metastatic testicular cancer, a condition his doctors thought was hopeless. He battled through his treatments and was back in competitive cycling in a little over one year. He won his first Tour de France at 27, and from then he became "a household name… a cause, a movement."[13]

A decade after, Armstrong's shining star plummeted when he publicly admitted that he used performance-enhancing drugs during his Tour de France wins. His fall would not have been so disgraceful if he had not repeatedly denied his teammates' allegations and demanded that they show proof. Proof came in 2012 when a USADA report ruled that he used illegal substances throughout most of his career. His public confession only came after he was stripped of his accomplishments and was publicly banned.[14] Armstrong believed he was "already excellent" because he was "praised for a virtue which is the opposite of [his] behavior," in Seneca's words, thus refusing to change his faulty behavior.

When one fails to acknowledge one's faults, Seneca's advice is to undergo introspection, essentially "claiming yourself for yourself (Vindica te tibi)."

 Our duty… will be, first, to examine our own selves, then the business we shall undertake, and lastly, those for whom or with whom we are undertaking it. Above all, it is necessary for a man to gauge himself accurately because we tend to think that we are able to do more than we really can… Some men because of their modesty are quite unsuited to public life, which calls for a confident front; some because of their unbending pride are not fitted for the courtroom; some do not have their anger under control; …some do not know how to restrain their sense of humour and cannot resist making a foolhardy joke.[15]

— SENECA, DE TRANQUILLITATE ANIMI,

6:1-2

On Self-Scrutiny And Self-Transformation

Introspection is the act of looking inward and examining oneself. Its aim is not to find blame or self-justification but to transform and make oneself new again. The task is not easy because it involves a confrontation between a person and his flawed past. As Seneca said:

 The value of the self is not something that is given, but that is the product of hard work. Some people have characters that are already virtuous or straightforward or are easily pliable to turn away from lives of vice and self-degradation. But there are others who "have to be worked on." The self is seen as a construction, and a struggle is necessary for the self to achieve victory (Vincere) "with the self as both victor and defeated."[16]

— SENECA

The struggle is a personal one, and for those who have practiced introspection before, it is necessarily a lonely trek. However, being alone with oneself is not advisable for those new to the practice of introspection, particularly if one has a troubled conscience. Seneca warns against the dangers of solitude for the inexperienced, for whom the guidance of a tutor or mentor is very important.[17]

A good conscience welcomes the crowd, but a bad conscience, even in solitude, is disturbed and troubled.[18]

— SENECA, LETTER 28

But Seneca consoles us with acknowledging that those who have led a flawed life and have much to regret are also those who have the most to gain from self-scrutiny and transformation.

> So I should refer to one who has never had any trouble with himself as more fortunate; but the other, I feel, has done better by himself, for he has conquered the twistedness of his own nature, and his road to wisdom has been not gentle but steep.[19]
>
> — SENECA, LETTER 52.6

On Emotions: We Should Always Keep Calm.

One of Seneca's most powerful lessons concerns the strength of our emotions and how we may control them. Of all the emotions, he particularly expounded on the uselessness of anger and, at the same time, its potential destructiveness. He differentiates acts guided by reason, even if they entail violence, from acts of anger.

> Of what use is anger, when the same end can be arrived at by reason? Do you suppose that a hunter is angry with the beasts he kills? Yet he meets them when they attack him, and follows them when they flee from him, all of which is managed by reason without anger. … Anger, therefore, is not useful even in wars

or battles: for it is prone to rashness, and while trying to bring others into danger, does not guard itself against danger. The most trustworthy virtue is that which long and carefully considers itself, controls itself, and slowly and deliberately brings itself to the front.[20]

— SENECA, ON ANGER, 1.11

Concerning anger, Seneca wrote, "We shouldn't control anger, but destroy it entirely – for what control is there for a thing that's fundamentally wicked?" [21]. That being said, this philosopher showed his pragmatic side when he acknowledged in another passage that people should learn to control anger before they can destroy it. He describes the process using a court trial as a metaphor.

When the day was over and [Sextius] had retired to bed, he would put these questions to his soul: "What faults of yours have you cured today? What vice have you resisted? In what way are you improved?" Anger will cease and become more controllable when it finds it has to appear before a judge every day. Can anything be more excellent than this piece of thoroughly examining the whole day?... I have adopted this strategy and every day I plead my cause before myself as judge.[22]

— SENECA, DE IRA (ON ANGER) 3.36.1-3

Thus, when self-examining our conduct at the end of the day, we call to judgment the emotions that motivate our actions. This daily exercise helps us to recognize the onset of anger and to bring it under control before it gains control of us.

On Self-Control

Seneca does not single out anger as the only emotion to be tempered, but all emotions lead a person to commit a fault.

> Every emotion at the start is weak. Afterwards it rouses itself and gains strength by progress; it is more easy to forestall it than to forgo it... Let us therefore resist these faults when they are demanding entrance, because, as I have said, it is easier to deny them admittance than to make them depart.[23]
>
> — SENECA, LETTER 116

Just as with anger, Seneca taught that when we recognize the onset of emotions that tend to lead us to commit fault or error, we can stop it before it takes hold of our actions, something easier to resolve than after the damage has been done.

However, anybody told to control their emotion before it begins will naturally reply, "That's easier said than done," or, "Emotions are too powerful; they cannot be controlled." To this, Seneca teaches:

> And do you know why we have not the power to attain this Stoic ideal? It is because we refuse to believe in our power. Nay, of a surety, there is something else which plays a part: it is because we are in love with our vices; we uphold them and prefer to make excuses for them rather than shake them off. We, mortals, have been endowed with sufficient strength by nature, if only we use this strength, if only we concentrate our powers and rouse them all to help us or at least not to hinder us. The reason is unwillingness, the excuse, inability.[24]

> — SENECA, LETTER 116

Roger Federer is a world tennis champion known for his calm, measured disposition and self-control. This was not always the case, however. Early in his career, Federer was known for his fits of anger on the court and his lack of concentration. He described his early years and the realization that he needed to change:

> I cried a lot, and I threw my rackets everywhere. When I lost, I even broke some of them; believe me, I had to do a lot to learn to control my behavior. The key moment of

my change was in 2001 in Hamburg. I lost a match I should have won, and my behavior was so bad that I was upset with myself, and that's where I decided to keep myself calm, and I did it; I would say I became too calm, which is why people were looking at me as a non-competitive guy… I did not know how to find a balance between the two mental states, the anger, and the calmness.[25]

— ROGER FEDERER

The event that ultimately shocked the young Federer to take control of his inner self was the death of his coach, Peter Carter, in a car accident a week before Federer's 21st birthday. Though he was devastated, this was the first time Roger suddenly faced his mortality. It became his wake-up call. He began to focus on his attitude and control his emotions, balancing his raging competitiveness with mental calm. He consulted a sports psychologist who counseled him for several years. [26] That inner resolve and hard work resulted in Federer's first Wimbledon win in 2003 and the Grand Slam dominance.

On Our Words: Speak Only Less But With Substance

 What is required is not a lot of words, but effectual ones.[27]

— SENECA, LETTER 38

Ever heard of the word "grandiloquence"? The dictionary describes this word as a combination of the Latin word grandis ("grand") and loquis ("speak"). From its etymology, you could guess that grandiloquence refers to "a type of talk that is pompous and bombastic" but expresses nothing of importance.[28] Just the definition certainly brings to mind many people you have come across. People who are grandiloquent are difficult to forget because they are often unnerving and annoying to the point that you would want to avoid their company.

On the other hand, some people speak only when necessary. One such person is the honorable Justice Clarence Thomas of the U.S. Supreme Court. For ten years, Justice Thomas did not speak a word from the Supreme Court bench, only quietly listening to the very complex arguments before it. But in February 2016, he broke his silence to ask a very important question from the lawyers debating before the court. It was such a profound event that the news carried the story, not of the case, but of Justice Thomas speaking for the first time in a decade.[29]

It seems that times have hardly changed since the years Seneca walked the earth. He said of some of his fellow philosophers:

> Ye Gods, what strength and spirit one finds in him! This is not the case with all philosophers; there are some men of illustrious name whose writings are sapless.

They lay down rules, they argue, and they quibble; they do not infuse spirit simply because they have no spirit. But when you come to read Sextius, you will say: "He is alive; he is strong; he is free; he is more than a man; he fills me with a mighty confidence before I close his book.[30]

— SENECA, LETTERS TO LUCILLIUS.

On Avoiding Things That Are Not Essential

> Living is the least important activity of the preoccupied man, yet nothing is harder to learn.[31]

— SENECA, ON THE SHORTNESS OF LIFE

Among Seneca's lessons, he extolled the virtues of living a simple life for its own merit and the benefit it brings. Often, we undertake the act of denying ourselves the luxuries of this world as some sort of punishment. Society regards basic living as insufficient while treating the luxurious lifestyle as the norm. Not so, according to Seneca. "Philosophy calls for simple living, not for doing penance, and the simple way of life need not be a crude one."[32] He explains why simple living is more beneficial even if one could afford more.

Reserve a few days in which we may prepare ourselves for real poverty by means of fancied poverty. There is all the more reason for doing this, because we have been steeped in luxury and regard all duties as hard and onerous. Rather let the soul be roused from its sleep and be prodded, and let it be reminded that nature has prescribed very little for us. No man is born rich. Every man, when he first sees light, is commanded to be content with milk and rags. Such is our beginning, and yet kingdoms are all too small for us.[33]

— SENECA

Seneca teaches that contrary to social thinking, it is simple living that is the ideal lifestyle. It is because the state of poverty is closer to the state every person is born to. By living on the basics, we are living closer to what nature had intended for us. Those who get accustomed to luxuries are bound to suffer greatly if their fortunes suddenly change and they lose their wealth and property. Those who live contented with less despite being rich will not fall into the trap of wanting more and more. As Seneca said, "It is not the man who has too little, but the man who craves more, that is poor."

On Constant Self-Improvement Through Leisure

A popular 1659 proverb credited to James Howell goes like this:

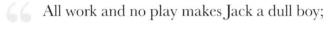

> All work and no play makes Jack a dull boy;
>
> All play and no work makes Jack a mere toy.[34]

The proverb has become so popular because it reflects the common concept that work and leisure are opposite and exclusive activities. The idiom conveys that work and play are both beneficial, but they can't be done together. So they must be balanced off because a person engaging too much in one tends to neglect the other.

Seneca, however, teaches that even leisurely activities afford people a chance to work towards improving themselves.

> This leisure is spent by a man so that he may (if possible) benefit many men; and if not, a few; if not then, those closest to him; and if not then, himself. For when he makes himself beneficial to the rest of society, he performs a public service (negotium).[35]
>
> — SENECA, LETTER 3

Leisure is still an undertaking in the same manner as work is an undertaking. We exert effort in both.

"Leisure" and "rest" to the Stoics were active pursuits. Leisure is therefore not idleness or rest, but activity with a goal. Seneca teaches that our efforts are devoted to attaining three goals–action, contemplation, and pleasure.

> There are three kinds of life, and the best of these is usually sought: one is devoted to pleasure, the second to contemplation, and the third to action… [A]ll three kinds of life – under this name or that – come to the same thing: he who sanctions pleasure is not without contemplation, he who is devoted to contemplation is not without pleasure, and he who sets his life for action is not without contemplation.[36]

> — SENECA, LETTER 7

Seneca said that even the man society would judge poorly, the one who pursues pleasure "does not value idle pleasure but achieves for himself by reason a pleasure which is steadfast."[37] There are many examples of people who pursue leisure for pleasure's sake but challenge themselves to achieve their best. The best examples of this are the people who seriously pursue hobbies – sports, the arts, homemaking, even something as mundane as keeping a collection of rare coins or stamps. Others are even communal, such as mentoring youths and undertaking civic work. These are leisure activities that enable us to work towards self-improvement while providing us much pleasure.

On Learning From Challenges

> I assume the spirit of a man who seeks where he may make trial of himself, where he may show his worth... I want something to overcome, something on which I may test my endurance. For this is another remarkable quality that Sextius possesses: he will show you the grandeur of the happy life and yet will not make you despair of attaining it; you will understand that it is on high, but that it is accessible to him who has the will to seek it."[38]

— SENECA, MORAL LETTERS TO
LUCILLIUS

Have you heard of No Barriers? It is an organization founded by Erik Weihenmayer, a middle-aged school teacher in the U.S. whose goal is to help disabled people complete challenges. The motto of No Barriers is, "What's within you is stronger than what's in your way." The motto may well be his own because Erik is the only blind person ever to reach the summit of Mt. Everest and scale the Seven Summits – the highest peak of every continent in the world. No Borders helps differently-abled individuals such as amputees, people living with Multiple

Sclerosis, and cancer survivors meet the challenges they set for themselves.

One of No Barriers' members, Mark Inglis, is the first double-amputee to climb Everest. When asked by reporters why he needed to climb the world's tallest mountain, he explained that he didn't do it for the acclamation. "It gives you the knowledge of empowerment to do other things." [39] Seneca understood this and explained that our limitations are a product of our perceptions. "We suffer more often in imagination than in reality." He also believed that "It does not matter what you bear, but how you bear it." Overcoming our limitations requires that we keep the prize in sight and summon up in ourselves the will to achieve it. How we eventually do so is the real achievement.

On The Shortness Of Life

 We're tight-fisted with property and money, yet think too little of wasting time, the one thing about which we should all be the toughest misers. [40]

— SENECA

We think of inventors or authors whose works have stood the test of centuries as bespectacled wizened men or women. They must have lived such long lives that they had enough time to gain enough wisdom to achieve such great accomplishments. If this was your thinking, the following inventors would come as a surprise to you, as well as the familiarity of their inventions:

- Frank Epperson, 11 years old, invented the popsicle in 1905;
- George Nissen, 16 years old, invented the trampoline in 1930;
- Chester Greenwood, 15 years old, invented the earmuffs in 1873;
- Joseph-Armand Bombardier, 15 years old, invented the snowmobile in 1922;
- Ben Franklin, 11 years old, invented the swim flippers in the early 1700s; and
- Louis Braille, 12 years old, invented – you guessed it - the Braille reading system for the blind in 1824. [41]

Furthermore, did you know that the author of the now-famous Frankenstein, Mary Shelley, wrote her novel when she was only 18 years old? Shelley published her book in 1817 during an era when women played a subordinate role in society, making her achievement doubly noteworthy. The lesson here is that a person's accomplishment is not time-bound if that person fills her waking hours with worthwhile pursuits. Therefore, one could do much even if life is short, and there is enough time to do everything necessary if one spends time wisely. Nature gives people enough time to do everything important, the essay goes, and should be allocated to accomplish what is vital in life. An intentional, purposeful life is one that is always lived in the present. In his letter to Lucillius, "On the Quality, as Contrasted with the Length, of Life," Seneca wrote:

> And what difference does it make how soon you depart from a place which you must depart from sooner or later? We should strive, not to live long, but to live rightly; for to achieve long life you have need of Fate only, but for right living you need the soul. A life is really long if it is a full life; but fullness is not attained until the soul has rendered to itself its proper Good. [42]… Pray, let us see to it, my dear Lucillius, that our lives, like jewels of great price, be noteworthy not because of their width but because of their weight. Let us measure them by their performance, not by their duration.[43]
>
> — SENECA, LETTER 93

Time well spent creates value for oneself and, as these children's accomplishments show, value for many generations to come. As Seneca observed when comparing a productive man versus an idle man: "The former exists even after his death; the latter had died even before he was dead."[44]

On The Value Of Having A Philosophy/ Stoicism

Fittingly, the last lesson in this brief discussion of Seneca's teachings delves into the value of having a philosophy in life. Philosophy is essentially the search for knowledge; Stoic philosophy is living that knowledge to attain happiness. In his letter entitled "On Philosophy, the Guide of Life," Seneca wrote:

> No man can live a happy life, or even a supportable life, without the study of wisdom; you know also that a happy life is reached when our wisdom is brought to completion, but that life is at least endurable even when our wisdom is only begun.[45]
>
> — SENECA. LETTER 16

It is a fundamental truth, which all of us know intuitively, that happiness means something different for each of us and can come only from within us.

> Do the one thing that can render you really happy: cast aside and trample underfoot all the things that glitter outwardly and are held out to you by another or as obtainable from another; look toward the true good, and rejoice only in that which comes from your own store. And what do I mean by "from

your own store"? I mean from your very self, that which is the best part of you.[46]

— SENECA, LETTER 23

We believe that happiness is what we aim for in life, and it directs all our actions and decisions. Not knowing what can bring us happiness is equivalent to not having a philosophy in life and absent from this, our actions and decisions become misguided and, therefore, meaningless.

> The archer must know what he is seeking to hit; then he must aim and control the weapon by his skill. Our plans miscarry because they have no aim. When a man does not know what harbor he is making for, no wind is the right wind.[47]

— SENECA, LETTER 71

Therefore, each person's happiness is uniquely his own, and it is by pursuing knowledge about himself and the world, he discovers what makes him happy. Only when he derives from his own philosophy the meaning of happiness for him will he be able to chart the course of his life that will lead to his true happiness.

Action Steps

Of all Seneca's teachings, probably the most relevant to today's hectic lifestyle is controlling one's emotions, particularly anger. In the heat of the moment, there is very little we can do to prevent passionate outbursts or impulsive acts. But there are three exercises Seneca taught his students, which can also help us control our emotions.

1. <u>Reflection at the start of the day</u> - Before going out to do your daily activities, take a moment to reflect on everything that can happen during that day. This does not mean simply planning what to do. It also involves trying to foresee the good and the bad, the intended and the unintended, and adopt the frame of mind that it is likely to happen. As Seneca said, "fortune has the habit of behaving as she pleases," so if you already expect something, it will come as less of a shock.

2. <u>Delay your reaction</u> - Let's say the unavoidable and undesirable event happens, and you feel the urge to react emotionally. If the emotion is negative and the reaction is something you will regret later on, train yourself to delay your reaction. Some people would say, count from one to ten and take a deep breath. It usually works.

3. <u>Take stock at the end of the day</u> - In an earlier chapter, we discussed journalling. This is consistent with the end-of-the-day reflection. Go over your actions for the day, and recall the moments you may have lost control of your emotions. Remember the feeling. Try to discern the tell-tale signs leading to the event. It will help you prepare for

any future recurrence of a similar situation, so you can take control before you lose it.

Moving On

Fortune is fickle, so if we lived according to what fortune deals us, then our lives would be like flimsy boats pitching about in perilous waves. Seneca's teachings in Stoicism are intended to be a lighthouse in the storm, guiding the boats to the harbor. Another Stoic philosopher built on the same principles and delivered them in his own creative style, as the next chapter will show us.

Chapter Summary

- Although many of Seneca's writings have disappeared through the centuries, a voluminous body of his work still survives to this day.
- Seneca teaches us that self-worth is not measured by wealth or possession but by the extent to which he lives a virtuous life.
- We must confront his flaws through honest introspection and a resolve to transform ourselves.
- It is important to control our emotions and develop a calmness towards whatever events may act according to what is best.
- In our words, deeds, and lifestyle, we must avoid the superfluous and keep to what is essential.

- Leisure, used actively, aids in self-improvement and accepting challenges to expand the limits of our abilities.
- Life, though short, is enough to accomplish all that is important in life. Therefore, we need a philosophy to guide our lives towards achieving what is important.

4

EPICTETUS – A SLAVE BECOMING THE MOST SOUGHT-AFTER STOIC PHILOSOPHER

> I was Epictetus, a slave, and maimed in body, and a beggar for poverty, and dear to the immortals.[1]

— EPICTETUS, DISC. III. 22. COMP. 1

One of the most loved fairy tales of all time is Cinderella. Authored by Charles Perrault, it tells of a girl treated like a servant who captivated a prince and became a princess. The story's appeal is its message of hope that people of limited means and low status may aspire to something better in the future. Such was the life of Epictetus, a crippled slave with a non-descript name. Despite having no pedigree, wealth, nor title, his legacy has survived the millennia and enshrined him as one of the world's most admired philosophers.

Early Life

Epictetus (55 – 135 CE) [2] was born in unknown
circumstances. His birthplace was most probably
Hierapolis, a city in Phrygia.[3] What little is known of his
life are a testament to his humble beginnings and the
remarkability of his eventual rise to acclaim as a
philosopher. Epictetus was born into poverty, and the
name his parents have given him is unknown. The name
he went by, the Greek word epíktētos (ἐπίκτητος),
translates to "acquired" or "gained." It is the term used
by Plato in his Laws to signify property that is annexed or
added to a person's inherited assets.[4]

When and how exactly Epictetus developed a thirst for
philosophy is difficult to determine from the sparse
historical accounts. However, it seems that his interest was
sparked at a young age, long before he was freed from
slavery.

It is believed that his slave beginnings (his mother was a
slave when she gave birth to him [5]) set the tone and
temper of his whole life, and fueled his passion for
independence and freedom.[6] It may be this passion that
drove the young Epictetus to learn about philosophy.

His owner was Epaphroditus, secretary to Nero and, after
Nero's death, to Domitian. Epictetus spent his youth in
Rome and had direct daily experience at the imperial
court, as may be inferred from his anecdotes about
persons who had business at the court. His master
permitted him to attend lectures by the renowned Stoic

philosopher Musonius Rufus.[7] Being schooled in this manner accorded him a higher social status. At about this time, however, Epictetus became crippled; it was alleged by Origen [8] that his leg was broken by his owner.[9] The following account is drawn from *Contra Celcus*.

> Might you not, then, take Epictetus, who, when his master was twisting his leg, said, smiling and unmoved, 'You will break my leg;' and when it was broken, he added, 'Did I not tell you that you would break it?'[10]

— ORIGEN

Before going further, it is possible that this account might not be true. Simplicius, a Neoplatonist philosopher, wrote that Epictetus had been lame from childhood.[11] But if Origen's account was true, it is an example of how Epictetus abided by his own teaching – that all external events are beyond our control and that we should calmly and dispassionately accept whatever may happen. With scrupulous self-discipline, we can learn to control our reactions and responses to uncontrollable events Thus, did Epictetus show his detachment and self-discipline even in this most extreme of circumstances.

Adult Life

Epictetus became a freedman sometime after Nero's death in 68 C.E., although he was lame and in ill health his whole life. After he attained his freedom, he began to teach philosophy in Rome. In about 90 C.E., the emperor Domitian expelled all philosophers from the city.[12]

Epictetus then settled in Nicopolis in Southern Epirus, Greece, and established his school of philosophy. He gathered around him a large group of pupils of various backgrounds and social statuses and instructed them much as Socrates had done in various public places through precept and example. Sometime in 117 C.E., it is said that the emperor Hadrian invited him back to Rome, but Epictetus declined.

In the scant literature dealing with the account of Epictetus' life, the only teacher of note mentioned to have taught him was Gaius Musonius Rufus, the first of the four great Stoic philosophers introduced in the first chapter of this book. While his mentor's Stoic principles most influenced him, Epictetus has imprinted his distinct insights when handing down his philosophy to his students.

Teaching Career

The teaching method and philosophy of Epictetus was handed down through the centuries by his student Flavius Arrian, through two of his principal works: The Discourses and The Handbook, around 104-107 C.E. Epictetus taught on all the three branches of Stoic philosophy, namely logic, physics, and ethics. However,

The Discourses and Enchiridion (Handbook) focused on ethics.

Some suggest that the two works, supposedly written by Arrian, were actually written by Epictetus himself, because according to the Suda, [13] Epictetus 'wrote a great deal." Also, many have called into question Arrian's claim in the preface of these works that they were written verbatim from Epictetus' extemporaneous discussions.[14] Unfortunately, there is no way to verify Epictetus' direct authorship of the works, but this is not significant for many philosophy students. Socrates himself did not write his own works; rather, his student Xenophon did. Thus, this is not new nor particularly concerning.

Later Life Until Death

Epictetus lived in great simplicity throughout his life. Unlike Seneca, who lived modestly but, in reality, was wealthy, Epictetus actually had very few possessions: a bed, a cooking vessel, and an earthen lamp. He discouraged marriage and procreation.[15] He had no wife or children of his own for most of his life, but he adopted the child of a friend who had no one else to care for him in his advanced age. Epictetus raised the child with the help of a woman who he may or may not have married.[16] He died of natural causes at about the year 135 C.E.

Action Steps

Epictetus' life was simple and uncomplicated. This is almost an impossibility in meeting the demands of our contemporary lifestyle. But we could try, if we wanted, to forego some excesses that we psychologically regard as essential. In 2018, the U.S. Bureau of Labor and Statistics researched what an average household spends its income on.[17] The average annual amounts spent on particular consumer good categories are:

- Food at home: $4,464
- Food away from home: $3,459
- Apparel and services: $1,866
- Vehicle purchases: $3,975
- Gasoline and other fuels: $2,109
- Personal care products and services: $768
- Entertainment: $3,226

Scanning through the list, it appears that households spend most on food, next on transportation, and third on entertainment. It must have come as a surprise that entertainment expenses are higher than apparel and services, considering that food, clothing, and shelter are humans' primary needs. It is also assumed that personal care products and services include toiletries, medicines, and visits to the doctor. Therefore, does this mean that entertainment is considered more essential than apparel, personal care, and the services that go with them?

Try listing down your household consumption expenses and rank them according to the amount. What are the consumption purchases that are most essential to you? Why do you consider them essential? Do you think you can do without some of them?

Moving On

Despite being poor and crippled, Epictetus declared himself "dear to the immortals." Far from being boastful, these words have turned out to be a statement of fact. He was indeed immortalized not only because of what he taught but because of how he exemplified his teachings. His life was unremarkable in the ways of the world because he conquered no countries nor amassed any wealth. But the brilliance of his teachings, which we discuss in the next chapter, inspired even the great Emperor Marcus Aurelius and have enshrined him in history.

Chapter Summary

- Epictetus was born to a slave mother, and his real name is not known. The word Epictetus which he was named for, translated to "acquired," signifying him as property.
- As a slave to Epaphroditus, secretary to Nero, Epictetus was exposed to the teachings of Roman philosophers. He was allowed to be

instructed by the Stoic philosopher Musonius Rufus.

- Epictetus gained renown as a philosopher and eventually was given his freedom. He taught philosophy in Rome until the emperor Domitian expelled all philosophers.
- He moved to Greece, where he taught philosophy. He became renowned and was invited back to Rome by the emperor Hadrian, but he declined the invitation.
- Epictetus continued to teach until his last days. His teachings have resulted in two works, The Discourses, and the Enchiridion.

5

EPICTETUS' DISCOURSES AND HANDBOOK: HIS TAKE ON STOICISM

Don't explain your philosophy. Embody it.[1]

— EPICTETUS

This saying by Epictetus is a favorite among inspirational speakers and leadership mentors today. We even have modern cliches that approximate it, like: "Put your money where your mouth is," and "Practice what you preach." Simple and straightforward, it strikes at the weakness of many modern leaders – the failure to follow their own declarations. Though he lived simply, Seneca was often criticized for not repudiating his wealth like the Cynics and is regarded by his detractors as a hypocrite. On the other hand, Epictetus was born into poverty and lived on the bare essentials for all of his life.

For Epictetus, Philosophy Was A Way Of Living

The former slave who gained his freedom and earned the respect of emperors and nobility lived the true life of a Stoic, characterized by great simplicity and humility. He embodied the central teaching of Stoicism, that is, to use reason to master oneself. It is only through this that a person may live a life of virtue in accordance with nature.[2]

Epictetus emphasized that the purpose of philosophy is to help people have a good and meaningful life. He, therefore, emphasized that practicing the principles is part of learning them. Self-knowledge is the key to self-control.

Epictetus' Focus On The Concept Of "Logos"

In all of Stoicism, the concept of *logos* is the force that guided the universe and moved all things and all people. So all-encompassing is the concept that some writers who eventually translated the ancient works often referred to *logos* in terms of God.[3] The principle behind *logos* was first articulated by Heraclitus (500 B.C.E.), the pre-Stoic philosopher who predated Socrates (discussed in Chapter 1). After Heraclitus, Antisthenes and then Zeno of Citium further developed the concept.

Under Epictetus, *logos* took on a clearer and more practical dimension. He focused on the responsibility of individuals to live the best life they possibly can. He portrays *logos* as "the underlying form of the perceived world which sets the parameters of the human experience and maintains the order of the universe by immutable laws."[4]

As individuals, we are limited by the natural operation of *logos* in the choices we can make. However, we retain the power to interpret our environment and how we may respond to it. The circumstances around us are not intrinsically pleasant or terrible; how we respond to them makes them so. An example is how Epictetus described death.

> Men are disturbed not by the things which happen, but by the opinions about the things: for example, death is nothing terrible, for if it were it would have seemed so to Socrates; for the opinion about death, that it is terrible, is the terrible thing.

> — EPICTETUS, ENCHIRIDION

An example in history of one such death is Jeanne d'Arc (Joan of Arc), whose military campaign turned the Hundred Years' War in favor of France. She was captured and sentenced to be burned at the stake for heresy. Just as she was to be executed by burning, which we all agree is a terrible death, 19-year-old Joan "instructed a priest to hold high a crucifix for her to see and to shout out prayers loud enough to be heard above the roar of the flames."[5] This is one of the more graphic examples of the truth Epictetus speaks about when saying that men's opinions color an event as good or bad. For Jeanne d'Arc's detractors, her death was a just execution. For the whole of Christendom, it was a martyrdom that was designed by Providence (i.e., *logos*).

While Epictetus affirmed that we must live according to *logos*, we must clarify that he did not mean that logos direct our choices as an outside force. Human choice is still governed by free will. We are accountable for how we conduct our affairs, and in fact, it is by accepting this responsibility that humans become free to act, to become masters of their own lives.

Epictetus Emphasized The Three *Topoi* (Aka Areas Of Study Or Disciplines) In Stoicism

According to Epictetus, there are three areas of study wherein the Stoic student may apply the principles they had learned – the disciplines of desire, action, and assent [6]. There are corresponding sets of exercises for *topoi* whereby the students may attain a happy life (*eudaemôn*) within the ability of rational beings to achieve.

Desires (*Orexeis*) And Aversions (*Ekkliseis*)

This area of study has to do with acceptance of our fate. According to the Stoics, only what is innately good and virtuous is worthy of desire. Virtuous living is abiding by *logos* which requires us to act on those things that are within our power to control and accept those not within our power to control.

> Of these [three areas of study], the principle, and most urgent, is that which has to do with the passions; for these are produced in no other way than by the disappointment of our desires, and the incurring of our aversions. It is this that introduces disturbances, tumults, misfortunes, and calamities; and causes sorrow, lamentation and envy; and renders us envious and jealous, and thus incapable of listening to reason.[7]

— EPICTETUS, DISCOURSES 3.2.3,
TRANS. HARD

According to Epictetus, this is a principal area of study because the things we desire become the anchors for our feelings of fulfillment; if we do not attain them, we feel frustration. "When I see a man anxious, I say, 'What does this man want?' If he did not want some thing which is not in his power, how could he be anxious?'" (Discourses 3.2.3) [8]. Epictetus felt so strongly about this that he called the afflictions brought about by "passions" to be mankind's only source of misery.[9]

Think about how relevant this is to our present lifestyle characterized as "Keeping up with the Joneses." We see our neighbor has a flashy new car, and we desire the same. But the neighbor may be a highly paid company executive; it is within his power to purchase luxurious things which most people earning an average wage could not. Desiring what is not attainable makes one bitter and envious for no good reason. Therefore, people who want to lead a happy life must control their desires to match only what they can attain. We must be content with what we can achieve.

Impulse To Act (*Hormas*) And Not To Act (A*phormas*)

The second area of study concerns the impulse to act or not act – i.e., the motivation behind action or non-action. This area has to do with philanthropy or love of mankind. Again, this requires a discernment of what is within our power to do. In deciding to take action, much of what we are required to do is defined by our relationships with other people. Epictetus makes the following observation:

 Appropriate acts are in general measured by the relations they are concerned with. 'He is your father.' This means that you are called upon to take care of him, give way to him in all things, bear with him if he reviles or strikes you.

'But he is a bad father.'

Well, have you any natural claim to a good father? No, only to a father.

'My brother wrongs me.'

Be careful then to maintain the relation you hold to him, and do not consider what he does, but what you must do if your purpose is to keep in accord with nature.[10]

— EPICTETUS, HANDBOOK 30, TRANS.
MATHESON

The actions we take towards others are frequently defined by how we feel towards the recipient of our actions. Epictetus' illustration of how his children should treat a bad father calls to mind a real-life account of how a husband murdered his wife in front of his children. He was imprisoned for a long time, and he was old and infirm when he was released. None of his children wanted to care for him, so he was accepted into the care of some charitable nuns. So, should the children have cared for him? Many of us would say, of course not. He killed his wife and abandoned his children to the care of others. But Epictetus would say that the man's children, now grown adults, must act to fulfill their natural obligation to the man who gave life to them. It is not the father's actions that compel the obligation, but the relationship between them. *Logos* (nature) imposes that obligation.

Freedom From Deception, Hasty Judgement, And Anything Else Related To Assents (*Sunkatatheseis*)

Assent, which deals with mindfulness of our judgments, is *sunkatatheseis*, which is the Greek word for "approve" or "agree" with something – in this case, an impression. The Discipline of Assent is an exercise in interpreting our impressions and judging them to either accept them as true or not.

> The third area of study has to do with assent, and what is plausible and attractive. For, just as Socrates used to say that we are not to lead an unexamined life [see Plato, Apology 38a], so neither are we to accept an unexamined impression, but to say, 'Stop, let me see what you are, and where you come from', just as the night-watch say, 'Show me your token.'[11]
>
> — EPICTETUS, DISCOURSES 3.12.14–15,
> TRANS. HARD

All of us are familiar with having the wrong impression about something or somebody. Estranged spouses perceive their partners differently when separated compared to when they got married. The boss who gladly hired an employee three months ago fired him today for falsifying his qualifications. We also misinterpret actions and events. Wars were fought because countries have misjudged each other's intentions. Harm and injury result from putting faith in the wrong impression.

> Make it your study to confront every harsh impression with the words, 'You are but an impression, and not at all what you seem to be.' Then test it by those rules that you possess; and first by this–the chief test of all–'Is it concerned with what is in our power or with what is not in our power?' And if it is concerned with what is not in our power, be ready with the answer that it is nothing to you.
>
> — (HANDBOOK 1.5, TRANS. MATHESON)

Epictetus says that we could avoid the problems that arise due to false impressions by confronting those impressions by properly evaluating them before we act on them. A person, thing, or event is not by itself good or bad; the Stoic philosophy requires that we look at something either as good or bad if it impacts us in a beneficial or harmful way. "If we acquire this habit, we shall make progress, for we shall never give our assent to anything but that of which we get a convincing sense-impression." (Discourses 3.8.1-5, trans. Oldfather) [12]

On The Dichotomy Of Control

This is the second time we encounter this phrase, the first being in Chapter 1. The Stoic practice associated with this tenet recognizes the things we can do and those we cannot change.

Some things are in our control and others not. Things in our control are opinion, pursuit, desire, aversion, and, in a word, whatever are our own actions. Things not in our control are body, property, reputation, command, and, in one word, whatever are not our own actions.

— EPICTETUS, ENCHIRIDION

If we try to do something about things beyond our control, we will only face defeat. On the other hand, "You may be unconquerable if you enter into no combat in which it is not in your own control to conquer." – Epictetus, Enchiridion 19 [13]. The key, therefore, is to choose the battles we can fight and avoid those we cannot.

By removing our desire from those things that are beyond our control, then we will find ourselves "free, happy, and undisturbed."[14] We need to focus only on our actions and perceptions; everything else is not within our control. And what is beyond our control should not be a source of anxiety or disappointment.

On Living A Virtuous Life: Character Is Key

In Stoic philosophy, *prohairesis* signifies "moral character," or the capacity for rational beings to make choices and intend the repercussions of their actions.[15] Sometimes *prohairesis* is equated to intention, volition, will, moral purpose, or choice. Properly translated, in Stoicism it is understood as rational choice.

Character is the key to virtuous living. The following are manifestations of how moral character may be practiced:

(1) Do what is right. Remain indifferent to negative criticisms. Ignore what other people may say to force you to react or deter you from doing what is right.

(2) Resist temptation by practicing self-control. Overcoming temptation is more satisfying than indulging in it.

(3) Avoid entertainment or idle discussion on trivial topics. Entertainment and mass politics is like Plato's allegory of the cave, watching shadows on the wall – what would be a reality to the prisoners chained to the wall, but far from actual reality.

(4) Avoid talking too much of yourselves since it may vex others who are listening. Also, avoid rude and vulgar conversations, and convey to others that you disapprove of such talk.[16]

On God

It is uncertain whether Epictetus met with Christians early in his career, as some sources claim he may have. Early Christian historians note that Epictetus' date and place of birth coincide with apostolic history. "He was a compatriot and contemporary of Epaphras, a pupil of Paul, and founder of Christian churches in that province.

There is a bare possibility that he had a passing acquaintance with him, if not with Paul himself."[17] Although Epictetus' notions of God mirror those of Christianity closely, there is no historical account of a direct contact between them. Epictetus' frequently used the terms "God," "the gods," and Zeus interchangeably in the Discourses. In the *Enchiridion*, he spoke of God as a ship's captain who summons us, his crew, to board the ship that sets off on the journey in the afterlife. God loans us everything we have, and we eventually return all to him – family, friends, and possessions.[18] The true Stoic can never blame God or find fault with Him.

> Will you be angry and discontented with the ordinances of Zeus, which he, with the Fates who spun in his presence the thread of your destiny at the time of your birth, ordained and appointed? (Discourses 1.12.25, trans. Hard)
>
> — (DISCOURSES 1.12.25, TRANS. HARD)

Rather than blame God, the true Stoic followers trust that God will lead them to the fate for which they are destined.

> Lead me, Zeus, and you too, Destiny,
>
> Wherever I am assigned by you;
>
> I'll follow and not hesitate,
>
> But even if I do not wish to,

Because I'm bad, I'll follow anyway.
(Handbook 53, trans. White = extract from
Cleanthes' Hymn to Zeus)

God has stationed us to a certain place and
way of life.

— (DISCOURSES 1.9.24, TRANS. DOBBIN)

The Stoic concept of God is not different from nature or divine providence that gives N order to the universe. Epictetus' concept of God seems to be farther from the Greeks' idea of Zeus and the gods of Olympus; rather, He is a breath, a force that orders everything in the entire cosmos with a rational control according to how things should be. It is a continuous process of revelation, from one moment to the next, and is so devised that people have in their possession everything that is needed to fulfill their destiny, so there is nothing that they can complain of or blame for the failure to achieve their destiny.

> And so, when you have received everything, and your very self, from Another [i.e., God], do you yet complain and blame the Giver, if He take something away from you?

> — (DISCOURSES 4.1.100–3, WITH
> OMISSIONS, TRANS. OLDFATHER)

On Living According To Nature

From the Stoic conception of God, Epictetus then proceeds to show how it is ethical to live according to the laws of nature. Each person follows nature by pursuing excellence. This concept, "pursuing excellence," means firstly, that a person acts according to his nature, what is within his power and control, and secondly, to accept what fate brings to him. For instance, an employer reprimands his employee because the work he turned in was not according to the standards set. The employee must not feel aggrieved and try to get even with his employer by intentionally ruining his work, after which he will only justify getting dismissed. It is part of the order of the cosmos that an employer corrects his employees' mistakes, and the employees comply with his corrections.

> It is circumstances (difficulties) which show what men are. Therefore, when a difficulty falls upon you, remember that God, like a trainer of wrestlers, has matched you with a rough young man. For what purpose? you may say. Why, that you may become an Olympic conqueror; but it is not accomplished without sweat. In my opinion no man has had a more profitable difficulty than you have had, if you choose to make use of it as an athlete would deal with a young antagonist.

— (DISCOURSES 1.24.1–2, TRANS. LONG)

God puts hardships in our paths, but He does so for a reason. It is to make us better, hone our skills, improve our judgment, and eventually perform better. Have you ever wondered how the math problems you struggled with so much in the first grade are so simple to solve in the fifth grade? And yet, you would not have advanced through the years without passing through the hurdles of the earlier years. The more challenges come our way, the more we should be thankful for them.

> To be instructed is this, to learn to wish that everything may happen as it does. And how do things happen? As the disposer [i.e., God] has disposed them. And he has appointed summer and winter, and abundance and scarcity, and virtue and vice, and all such opposites for the harmony of the whole; and to each of us he has given a body, and parts of the body, and possessions, and companions.
>
> Remembering then this disposition of things, we ought to go to be instructed, not that we may change the constitution of things, – for we have not the power to do it, nor is it better that we should have the power, – but in order that, as the things around us are what they are and by nature exist, we may maintain our minds in harmony with the things which happen.

Epictetus acknowledges that there will always be situations that may potentially thwart us (e.g., scarcity and vice even as there are abundance and virtue). These situations are beyond our control. To remain consistent with nature, we should address the elements that are within our control. A father who loses his child in an unavoidable school bus accident may irrationally blame the driver. He may try to take revenge by litigating the case in court for years, then eventually lose anyway. Or he can accept that his child could not be brought back to life and devote his energies towards helping ensure that a similar accident does not happen again. One must trust in divine providence and be content in what fate has in store.

 The wise and good man … submits his own mind to him who administers the whole [i.e., God], as good citizens do to the law of the state. He who is receiving instruction ought to come to be instructed with this intention, How shall I follow the gods in all things, how shall I be contented with the divine administration, and how can I become free? For he is free to whom every thing happens according to his will [prohairesis], and whom no man can hinder.

On The Metaphors Of Life

Some of Epictetus' thoughts were so profound that he resorted to metaphors to convey to his students the Stoic lifestyle he envisioned. Five metaphors are discussed here.

Life As A Festival

> Who are you, and for what purpose have you come? Was it not he [i.e., God] who brought you here? … And as what did he bring you here? Was it not as a mortal? Was it not as one who would live, with a little portion of flesh, upon this earth, and behold his governance and take part with him, for a short time, in his pageant and his festival?
>
> — (DISCOURSES 4.1.104, TRANS. HARD)

Essentially, life is a celebration to which God invites us. We come not only as guests but as participants in the grand event. As with all happenings, there are pitfalls and difficulties, but these are only coincidental to the greater spectacle we must contribute to ourselves to fully enjoy the celebration. The key lesson here is that life is joyful! We should always search for those elements that make our lives happy.

. . .

Life As A Game

> To summarize: remember that the door is open. Do not be more cowardly than children, but just as they say, when the game no longer pleases them, 'I will play no more,' you too, when things seem that way to you, should merely say, 'I will play no more,' and so depart; but if you stay, stop moaning.
>
> — (DISCOURSES 1.24.20, TRANS. HARD;
> SEE ALSO 1.25.7–21 AND 2.16.37)

Games are played for our enjoyment, and for them to be challenging rules must guide them. The rules make the game sensible and interesting. But for the game to work and be enjoyable, everybody must play by a single set of rules.

This is just what you will see doing those who play at ball skillfully. No one cares about the ball as being good or bad, but about throwing and catching it. In this therefore is the skill, in this the art, the quickness, the judgment, so that even if I spread out my lap I may not be able to catch it, and another, if I throw, may catch the ball. But if with perturbation and fear we receive or throw the ball, what kind of play is it then, and wherein shall a man be steady, and how shall a man see the order in the game? But one will say, "Throw;" or "Do not throw;" and another will say, "You have thrown once." This is quarrelling, not play. (Discourses, 2.5) [19]

There is a popular expression: "I'm going to take my ball and go home!" The expression comes from a story where one kid (let's call him Joe) is playing a game – say basketball – with other kids. Joe does not like the way the game is going because it looks like he is about to lose fairly. It so happens that Joe owns the basketball. Just as he's about to lose, Joe gets the ball and takes it out of play. He says, "I'm going to take my ball and go home," abruptly ending the game in a manner that is contrary to the rules. The joy is gone, the other players are dismayed and maybe resentful of Joe, and the spectators are all disappointed at not seeing the game end. If Joe continued to play the game, he may have lost, but he might also have turned the game around and won. Either would have been his fate. But by taking the ball home, Joe will never know what his fate should have been.

Life As A Play

 Remember that you are an actor in a play, which is as the author [i.e., God] wants it to be: short, if he wants it to be short; long, if he wants it to be long. If he wants you to act a poor man, a cripple, a public official, or a private person, see that you act it with skill. For it is your job to act well the part that is assigned to you; but to choose it is another's.

Those of us who know a bit of Shakespeare would find this metaphor familiar. Life is a play, we are all actors, and God is the author. The famous soliloquy of the tragic hero goes:

 Life is but a walking shadow, a poor player that struts and frets his hour upon the stage, and then is heard no more. It is a tale told by an idiot, full of sound and fury, signifying nothing.

— WILLIAM SHAKESPEARE, MACBETH

Epictetus also thought of life as a play, but not in such dismal terms as in Macbeth. Shakespeare's actor is a shadow who just walks in the steps of others before him, and his life is a meaningless story. Epictetus' play, however, is one unique for every individual — we each play the role the author (God) wants us to play. We each act out the role we were given, and we should do so skillfully. That is our task. But we do not get to choose our roles, just as we do not choose our birth and upbringing circumstances.

From this metaphor, it appeared that Epictetus believed in fatalism and that there is nothing we can do about the cards we are dealt with. But the next metaphor shows that such is not the case.

. . .

Life As Weaving

In this metaphor, the wool that the weaver uses to make cloth takes the place of the ball in the game; that is, whatever material comes our way, it is our duty to make proper use of it, and if possible, make it into the best thing of its kind as we can (see *Discourses* 2.5.21–2).

 For we ought by all means to apply our art to some external material, not as valuing the material, but whatever it may be, showing our art in it. Thus, too, the weaver does not make wool, but exercises his art upon such as he receives.[20]

— DISCOURSES 2.5.21-2.

"We show our art" in the material, Epictetus says. Although we may not have a say in the material we are given, it is our art that we weave on it. Likewise, although we may not have a say in the circumstances of our birth, it is up to us to make the most of the life God gave us to live. Much like Epictetus himself, the philosopher was born a slave but has made his life so consequential that he influenced how people think to this day.

Life As An Athletic Contest

For is not reading a kind of preparation for living, but living itself made up of things other than books? It is as if an athlete, when he enters the stadium, should break down and weep because he is not exercising outside. This is what you were exercising for; this is what the jumping-weights, and the sand and your young partners were all for. So are you now seeking for these, when it is the time for action? That is just as if, in the sphere of assent, when we are presented with impressions, some of which are evidently true and others not, instead of distinguishing between them, we should want to read a treatise On Direct Apprehension.

— (DISCOURSES 4.4.11–13, TRANS. HARD)

The comparison between life and an athletic contest is quite obvious concerning the competition among players. But Epictetus emphasizes here the difference between training sessions and the actual competition. It is one thing to know the theory and to prepare for life, but another thing to get down to the business of living. We spend months and years learning, practicing, and training. But when called for, at any time and within a split second, we must be ready to apply what we have trained for in real life.

> Therefore, take the decision right now that you must live as a full-grown man, as a man who is making progress; and all that appears to be best must be to you a law that cannot be transgressed. And if you are confronted with a hard task or with something pleasant, or with something held in high repute or no repute, remember that the contest is now, and that the Olympic games are now, and that it is no longer possible to delay the match, and that progress is lost and saved as a result of one defeat and even one moment of giving in.
>
> — (DISCOURSES 4.4.11–13, TRANS. HARD)

Much as an athlete spends years in training, we spend a long time preparing for life. But just as the athlete faces the Olympics with readiness and resolve. When the learning and training are not undertaken with commitment, the athlete can only expect to show a poor performance when the contest takes place. Also, failure to study well and contemplate will fail in the way we conduct our lives.

Life As Military Service

> Do you not know that life is a soldier's service? One man must keep guard, another go out to reconnoitre, another take the field.

It is not possible for all to stay where they are, nor is it better so. But you neglect to fulfil the orders of the general and complain, when some severe order is laid upon you; you do not understand to what a pitiful state you are bringing the army so far as in you lies; you do not see that if all follow your example there will be no one to dig a trench, or raise a palisade, no one to keep night watch or fight in the field, but every one will seem an unserviceable soldier.

This metaphor conveys a more authoritarian power that God wields over man. The Stoic principle supporting this metaphor is that God governs the universe, and we are in His service whether or not we like it. Like a good soldier, a Stoic must discharge this service to the best of his ability without question. Therefore, it is not the place of a virtuous person to ask why some things happen and others do not. We are here to do God's bidding just as soldiers discharge the orders of their general.

 … So too it is in the world; each man's life is a campaign, and a long and varied one. It is for you to play the soldier's part–do everything at the General's bidding, divining his wishes, if it be possible.

— (DISCOURSES 3.24.31–5, TRANS. MATHESON; SEE ALSO 1.9.24 AND 1.16.20–1)

Action Steps

The Questioning Exercise

Epictetus was not mincing words when he said that philosophy should be practiced. He discussed the theory behind his lessons and gave practical exercises to actualize the process of living one's philosophy. One of these was the questioning exercise, as dubbed by Tremblay.[21] It involves answering a series of questions when one encounters an impression.

In the same way we exercise ourselves to deal with sophistical questioning, we should exercise ourselves daily to deal with impressions; for these too put questions to us, 'So-and-so's son is dead. What do you think of that?' It lies outside the sphere of choice, it is not an evil. – 'So-and-so has been disinherited by his father. What do you think of that?' It lies outside the sphere of choice, it is not an evil. – 'Caesar has condemned him.' – This lies outside the sphere of choice, it is not an evil. – He has been distressed by this. – This is within the sphere of choice, it is an evil. – He has borne it nobly. – This is within the sphere of choice, it is a good. (Discourses 3.8.1-3) [22]

To see how this is done, first select an event or situation in your day that has struck you as impressionable. Say, as you were crossing the street at the crosswalk, a car comes up at a fast clip and screeches to a halt. For a moment you were scared out of your wits. The driver sticks his head out of the window and shouts his apology. Thinking he was cursing at you, you respond by cursing back at him.

Applying the questioning exercise will yield the following analysis:

(1) You were crossing the street at the crosswalk. This lies within your control. It is a good.

(2) You were nearly hit by a car. This lies outside your control. It is neither a good nor an evil.

(3) The driver shouted his apology to you. This lies outside your control. It is neither a good nor an evil.

(4) You cursed at the driver. This is within your control. It is an evil.

In our conventional thinking, we would normally consider that you may have been hit by a car as an evil. But actually, since there is nothing you could have done to prevent it, the event is nothing more than the workings of *logos*. It was bound to happen and is, therefore, neither good nor evil. So was the reaction of the driver. But when you curse the driver, that is an evil because you had the choice to do it or not. It does not matter that you were scared half out of your wits at being nearly killed. Acting on your fear is a response of an irrational being; all animals would have been scared and reacted to defend itself. But Stoicism holds that we are rational beings and as such should act to attain excellence within the sphere of our control. You cannot blame the driver because doing so would be tantamount to blaming God. Even if you thought he might have cursed you, the good act would have been to respond benignly, as difficult as it would have been.

Now, try the exercise with another situation in your normal day. You might be surprised at how Epictetus' questioning exercise may enlighten you to act and think differently.

Moving On

"Don't explain your philosophy. Embody it." Words are not needed when one can show by deed the values one believes in. Philosophy is the pathway to happiness, and by living its tenets one achieves his life's fulfillment. It was said that the third pillar of Stoicism, Marcus Aurelius, embodied many of the principles Epictetus taught, both in his life and teachings. The next chapter will tell of both.

Chapter Summary

- Epictetus regarded philosophy as a way of life; learning Stoicism is inconsequential if not put into practice.
- In Epictetus' view, living a Stoic life requires complying with *logos* which is the divine providence that moves the cosmos.
- Epictetus taught that there are three topoi or areas of study in Stoicism: the disciplines of desire, action, and assent.
- For Epictetus, the dichotomy of control states that some things are within our control while other things are beyond it.

- Character is key to a virtuous life, and God is beyond all blame, according to Epictetus.
- Epictetus also described life as a series of metaphors, particularly a festival, a game, a play, weaving, an athletic contest, and military service.

6

MARCUS AURELIUS – THE RELUCTANT
AND THE LAST GOOD EMPEROR

Everything, a horse, a vine, is created for some duty. For what task, then, were you yourself created? A man's true delight is to do the things he was made for.[1]

— MARCUS AURELIUS

Have you heard the phrase, "Ours is not to reason why, ours is but to do or die"? It comes from The Charge of the Light Brigade, the poem for which Alfred Lord Tennyson is probably most famous for. Curiously, the poem celebrates what should be a tragic event – a suicidal cavalry charge during the Crimean war where 110 died and another 160 wounded out of 670 soldiers. The poem makes it clear at the onset that the cavalry's mission is a doomed one, without a chance of success, but the soldiers followed orders down to the last man. Thus, the immortal passage from the poem:

> "Forward, the Light Brigade!"
> Was there a man dismayed?
> Not though the soldier knew
>   Someone had blundered.
> Theirs not to make reply,
> Theirs not to reason why,
> Theirs but to do and die.
> Into the valley of Death
>   Rode the six hundred.
> -Alfred, Lord Tennyson, 1854 [2]

While the poem's most famous lines are the sixth and seventh in this second stanza, the more tragic phrase covers the third and fourth lines: "Not though the soldier knew Someone had blundered." It was known to the soldiers who were about to charge the cannons to the right, left, and front of them, armed only with sabers, that this was a glaring strategic error by the officer who commanded this mission. Nevertheless, not one soldier questioned their mission. They obeyed, and almost half of them were mortally wounded or killed. It was not so much because they were brave but because they remained loyal to their sense of duty.

The opening lines in this chapter reveals how he viewed a man's duty as "the thing he was made for" Marcus Aurelius demonstrated a keen perception of the need to fulfill one's duty. Man was made for a purpose. According to Stoic philosophy, man is a creature of nature, the cosmos, logos. But Marcus Aurelius, in his writings, brings man's existence closer to the work of divine Providence, a divine Creator who imbued man with a purpose. In this chapter, we explore the life of the pagan emperor who came closest to Christian teaching.

Early History

Marcus Aurelius was born in the fourth year of the emperor Hadrian's reign, on April 26, 121. His family was wealthy and politically prominent. His father was the praetor Marcus Annius Verus, nephew of Emperor Hadrian. He is said to have descended from Numa, the second King of Rome. His mother was the heiress Domitia Calvilla, "a lady of consular and kingly race." [3] His father died when he was three years old, after which his mother and grandfather raised him.

He was afforded a good education and studied Latin and Greek under such auspicious tutors as Herodes Atticus and Marcus Cornelius Fronto. His greatest intellectual interest, however, was in Stoic philosophy. He was particularly fascinated by the writings attributed to the humble slave and Stoic teacher by the name of Epictetus. The Discourses exerted much influence over Marcus Aurelius and his ideas on fate, reason, and control over one's emotions.

Adult Life And Ascendancy To The Throne

In the year 138 CE, when Marcus Aurelius was 17 years old, the adoptive son and heir to Emperor Hadrian, Aelius Caesar, died. To secure a successor, Hadrian adopted Marcus' uncle Antoninus Pius, who adopted Marcus and Lucius, the son of Aelius. It was said that Hadrian himself arranged for Antoninus to adopt Marcus and Lucius. Antoninus ascended the throne and became emperor upon the death of Hadrian. During the years 140, 145, and 161, Marcus served as Roman consul – i.e., the leader of the senate.

As time passed, Marcus was assigned more responsibilities and official powers and continued to study law and philosophy. Eventually, he grew to become a strong source of support and advice for Antoninus. He married Faustina, daughter to Antoninus, in the year 145. His marriage cemented the relationship between Marcus and Antoninus, further ensuring Marcus' position as heir apparent to the throne.

There was no indication that Marcus aspired to be emperor, but he definitely was prepared for it. He loved his adoptive father deeply, and he praised him profusely in his Meditations. During the 23 years Antoninus Pius reigned, Marcus devoted unswerving loyalty to him. As the years passed and Antoninus aged, Marcus assumed more of the emperor's duties, effectively and outwardly acting as co-emperor, although he did not possess the title. By March 161 CE, Marcus was already effectively discharging the duties of emperor, as Antoninus contracted a high fever and was confined to his family estate in Lorium. The account of his passing was a moving testament to his deep love for his beloved successor:

 Marcus rushed to be at his side. He charged Marcus with the care of both his daughter Faustina and of Rome, asked his attendants to move his golden statue of Fortune from his bedside to Marcus's, and then rolled over as if to sleep and quietly died, ending a reign of unprecedented peace in the Roman Empire. [4]

Upon the death of Antoninus, Caesar Marcus Aurelius Antoninus Augustus became the emperor of Rome. He was the last of the "Five Good Emperors," as Niccolo Machiavelli called them about 13 centuries later. The Five Good Emperors were Nerva (96-98 CE), Trajan (98-117 CE), Hadrian (117-138 CE), Antoninus (138-161 CE), and Marcus Aurelius (161-180). They presided over the Roman Empire during its most resplendent years (96 to 180 CE), succeeding Domitian (of evil fame) who died in the year 96 CE. . Their rule was said to be "the only period in history in which the happiness of a great people was the sole object of government." [5]

Marcus and Faustina had at least 12 children together, of whom five daughters and one son, Commodus, survived to adulthood. Commodus and his sister Lucilla rose to prominence in the years after Marcus died. Commodus succeeded as emperor, and Lucila conspired in a failed plot to assassinate her brother.

Main Character Traits

From historical accounts, Marcus Aurelius was a serious and hard-working student, traits that caught Emperor Hadrian's eye. He had a true love of learning and devoted himself to the search for intellectual fulfillment and the purity of life. He had a deep and abiding love for his tutors, particularly Marcus Cornelius Fronto, who remained a close friend and correspondent and upon whom he conferred many honors. He also showed intellectual humility, receiving instructions from Apollonius on Stoic philosophy even as an emperor. He was also a merciful ruler; when his general, Avidius Cassius, and his wife Faustina were involved (though inadvertently) in a plot to overthrow him, he readily forgave them. He mourned the loss of Cassius when his men turned on him and killed him, lamenting:

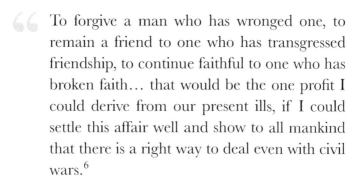

> To forgive a man who has wronged one, to remain a friend to one who has transgressed friendship, to continue faithful to one who has broken faith… that would be the one profit I could derive from our present ills, if I could settle this affair well and show to all mankind that there is a right way to deal even with civil wars.[6]

— MARCUS AURELIUS

Marcus embodied the principles that he taught. He observed the four cardinal virtues. The direct English translation from their Latin equivalents is prudence, temperance, fortitude, and justice. Their true connotations, however, differ from the English translations. "Prudence" is closer to wisdom, as "Justice" is to righteousness. "Fortitude" signifies manliness, courage, magnanimity, and love of honor. But the most important and all-encompassing of the four virtues is "Temperance," which means decorum, propriety, and conduct becoming of a gentleman. Temperance is "the most delicate and the most sophisticated of the virtues. [It] implies a sense of fitness, consideration, carefulness, reasonableness, a readiness to give to each his due. In fact, it borrows freely from the other virtues, for it is impossible to imagine perfect propriety without wisdom, courage or righteousness." [7]

Above all, more than the ancient philosophers before him, Marcus Aurelius taught love of neighbor. Stoicism emphasized the observance of ethics following logos to attain virtue and excellence. Marcus Aurelius refined this principle and elevated it to an act that approaches (though is not categorically equated with) Christian charity. To do a kind act towards others is the purpose for which we are created.

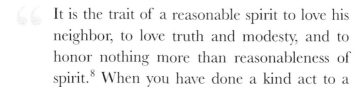

It is the trait of a reasonable spirit to love his neighbor, to love truth and modesty, and to honor nothing more than reasonableness of spirit.[8] When you have done a kind act to a man, what more do you want? Isn't it enough that you have acted in accord with your own nature? Are you looking for a reward for your act? As if the eye should ask to be paid for seeing, or the feet for walking? For just as eyes and feet were made for a particular service, and by doing that particular service come into their own, so a man was created by nature to do good; and when he has done a good action, or something that contributes to the general good, he has done what nature created him to do, and he has come into his own.[9]

— MARCUS AURELIUS

The Reign Of Marcus Aurelius

The reign of Marcus is marked by military conflict and conquests. Based on this characterization, one would have thought that he was well-schooled in military affairs, as would have been typical of the young, upcoming nobles. But Marcus had not been provided any military education by Pius, and therefore was unprepared in leading any military campaigns. He did not have the advantage of Antoninus, his predecessor, who spent 23 years ruling in the provinces.

The year he acceded to the throne, the Kingdom of Armenia, a Roman client state, was invaded by Vologases IV of Parthia. Almost simultaneously, there were threats of war in Britain. Likewise, in 162, in Raetia and Upper Germany. The Chatti of Taunus, long-standing enemies of Rome since the time of Domitian in 84 CE, again attempted to invade Romanian territory. To oversee these military engagements, Marcus' co-emperor Lucius Verus acted as the supreme commander of the Roman legion and conducted the military operations in the field. He was better qualified for the job, stronger than Marcus, and more physically fit for military life.

Marcus, older and in poorer health than his younger co-emperor, was better suited to Rome's domestic affairs. With his intelligence, character, and experience assisting Antoninus Pius, Marcus Aurelius became the ideal administrator and statesman. He introduced political reforms that earned for him the goodwill of the people. He added more court days and personally oversaw many of the cases. He introduced laws that extended protection towards orphans and children, expanded the formal emancipation of slaves, and strengthened the laws in the choosing of city officials. He greatly respected the Senate and consulted with them personally on many issues and proposals he wanted to pursue.

Marcus managed the empire's resources frugally, modified tax collection, and reduced wasteful spending such as the games and other forms of public entertainment. He instead invested more in welfare programs for the poor and compelled rich officials to invest some of their wealth back in the empire. He turned away informers and those who tried to bribe him. He was a temperate and benevolent leader who actively pursued justice and compassion, particularly for the less fortunate.

Tragedies

In 162 CE, a year after Marcus Aurelius and Lucius Verus ascended to the imperial throne, Rome was flooded when heavy rains inundated the Tiber, causing it to overflow its banks. So great was the flood that it brought immense damage to homes, property, and the agricultural estates in the surrounding countryside. Many of the livestock were drowned, and famine soon followed. By sheer will and personal sacrifice towards the resolution of the crisis, Rome recovered with relative speed. Marcus and Lucius personally attended to the needs of the people and spent a large portion of their own personal wealth to alleviate the disasters' adverse effects. By doing so, they won the love and respect of the Romans.

At about the same time, there was unrest among the Parthians in Syria, while other smaller wars broke out. Many of these encounters involved an element of cruelty and debauchery due to the disgraceful behavior of the generals and even Lucius Verus himself, who was renowned for his vices. But Marcus did not appear to have a direct hand in this. For the most part, he remained in Rome occupied with matters of law, adjudicating disputes and petitions.

After the wars, however, soldiers returning to Rome brought the plague with them. The illness, which might have been smallpox or measles, killed about five million. Simultaneous with the epidemic, the Germanic tribes intruded into Roman territory in the north. Roman military forces needed to defend their land, but Marcus joined Lucius to command the legions. It was uncertain whether this was because the mission was more difficult or because Marcus felt the need to oversee his brother's rowdy conduct. However, at the point of encounter, the Germanic tribes sued for peace, the matter was quickly settled, and the two emperors returned to Rome.

On the way home from this last campaign in 169 CE, Lucius Verus fell ill. He likely contracted the Antonine plague, which broke out in 165 CE and then spread throughout the land. He died in the carriage as Marcus tended to him. There were historical accounts, one of which was by Cassius Dio, that Marcus had Lucius killed because Lucius was suspected of planning to assassinate his brother. The accounts are doubtful; in truth, Lucius' death was a personal tragedy for Marcus because they had a genuine affection for each other even though they were very different.[10] The death of Lucius left Marcus Aurelius the sole emperor of Rome for the next 15 years.

Another tragedy attributed to the reign of Marcus Aurelius was the persecution of the Christians. The Christians enjoyed relative peace and freedom under the reign of Antoninus Pius, but apparently, they were violently persecuted under Marcus. The accusations against him were that he persecuted Christians, deliberately issued edicts against them, and that he sanctioned their oppression. But these charges were made by more recent writers, particularly John Foxe in his work, *Book of Martyrs*, published in 1563. Many modern writers dispute Foxe's charges against Marcus, noting that he did not cite his sources in his book. He described the persecutions in this manner:

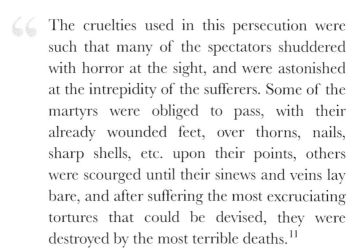

> The cruelties used in this persecution were such that many of the spectators shuddered with horror at the sight, and were astonished at the intrepidity of the sufferers. Some of the martyrs were obliged to pass, with their already wounded feet, over thorns, nails, sharp shells, etc. upon their points, others were scourged until their sinews and veins lay bare, and after suffering the most excruciating tortures that could be devised, they were destroyed by the most terrible deaths.[11]

— MARCUS AURELIUS

Foxe's account is regarded as false, not only because they lacked sources but also contradicted writings contemporary with Marcus Aurelius' reign. The ancient Christian apologists and writers who included Justin Martyr, Melito, Athenagoras, and others during the reign of Marcus Aurelius demonstrated "almost infinite trust in him and simply do not show any belief that he was a persecutor." [12] Tertullian (155-220 CE), one of the most prolific early Christian authors from Carthage, even adamantly declared Marcus Aurelius a protector of the Christians. Some modern historians, such as Donald Robertson [13], were quick to point out the writings of Irenaeus, Bishop of Lyons: "Through their [the Romans'] instrumentality the world is at peace, and we walk on the highways without fear, and sail where we will." [14] The ancient writers would not have written about Marcus in such favorable terms if he were truly the persecutor of Christians.

Death And Succession

Marcus Aurelius was already advanced in age when the Germanian tribes again launched an invasion into the northern Roman territory. Lucius Verus, Marcus' brother, and co-emperor, was already dead by this time, therefore Marcus was compelled to lead the military campaign against the invasion. The campaign was successful, although it appeared to have taken a toll on Marcus whose health was already frail from the beginning.

On the way home from the campaign, the emperor suffered a serious illness. While they were situated in the military camp at Vindobona, Marcus' health began to fail rapidly. Sensing that he may no longer recover, he realized that Commodus, his son, was about to become sole emperor while he was only 18. Marcus grew troubled that his son may fall into drinking and debauchery, forget his father's admonitions to study and remain virtuous, and instead mimic the former despots such as Dionysus, Nero and Domitian. His enemies may also take advantage of his son's youth and inexperience, and seize power for themselves.

When Marcus felt his end was near, he summoned his friends and kinsmen. He also called for Commodus, who he assigned to be his co-emperor since 176 CE. Placing his son before those assembled, he raised himself slightly on his couch, and spoke to them in the following manner:

> Here is my son, whom you yourselves have educated, approaching the prime of youth and, as it were, in need of pilots for the stormy seas ahead. I fear that he, tossed to and fro by his lack of knowledge of what he needs to know, may be dashed to pieces on the rocks of evil practices. You, therefore, together take my place as his father, looking after him and giving him wise counsel…
>
> When a man holds absolute power, it is difficult for him to control his desires. But if you give my son proper advice in such matters and constantly remind him of what he has heard here, you will make him the best of emperors for yourselves and for all, and you will be paying the greatest tribute to my memory. Only in this way can you make my memory immortal.[15]

— MARCUS AURELIUS

With these words, Marcus sank back on his couch in weakness. The following day, on March 17, 180 CE, he finally succumbed to his illness. When the news of his death spread, the entire army and the citizens of Rome grieved; as Robertson wrote, "No one in the Roman empire received the report without weeping. All cried out in a swelling chorus, calling him 'Kind Father,' 'Noble Emperor,' 'Brave General,' and 'Wise, Moderate Ruler,' and every man spoke the truth." [16]

Action Steps

The most important lesson we could derive from the life of this emperor-philosopher is his sense of duty. This chapter began with a memorable passage from Marcus' Meditations on this very theme. It is quite appropriate that the account of his life also ends with this theme. Of the three philosophers we have discussed, only Marcus Aurelius was in the position to put into practice every element of his philosophy. As emperor, he possessed an enlightened vision and unlimited political power. He had the opportunity to externalize the Stoic sense of duty more than the first two. In his Meditations he wrote:

 No matter what anyone says or does, my task is to be good. Like gold or emerald or purple repeating to itself, 'No matter what anyone says or does, my task is to be emerald, my color undiminished.'[17]

— MARCUS AURELIUS

Building on this, think of the most recent leadership position you personally held. You may have been a manager in your company, an officer in the military, or an official in government. You may be a teacher or parent. List down the duties of your leadership position. Thereafter, list the instances you *failed* to accomplish your duty. What were your reasons? Did you think they were justified at the time? Do you still think they are justified now? If you were to encounter similar circumstances in the future, what would you do differently?

Moving On

Generous, lenient, merciful, gentle, frugal, intelligent, skilled administrator – these were the words by which ancient historians, Roman pagan and Christian alike, described Marcus Aurelius. He was the leader of the most powerful empire of his time and possibly in all of history, but he discharged his duties with humility and dedication. His actions earned him the love of his people. His Stoic teachings, which we shall discuss in the next chapter, comprise his legacy for ages to come.

Chapter Summary

- Marcus Aurelius grew up in a politically prominent family and was tutored by auspicious scholars. His greatest interest was in Stoic philosophy.

- He succeeded his adoptive father, Antoninus Pius, as emperor of Rome in 161 CE. His sole condition was that his adoptive brother Lucius Verus ruled with him.
- As an emperor, he ruled with justice and mercy, observing the four cardinal virtues of prudence, temperance, fortitude, and justice.
- During their reign, Marcus Aurelius focused on the administration of the empire while his brother and co-emperor Lucius Verus took charge of the military campaigns to secure the empire. Lucius Verus died of the plague in 169 CE.
- Marcus ruled wisely until he died in 180 CE; thereafter, he was succeeded by his youthful son, Commodus.

7

THE MEDITATIONS OF MARCUS AURELIUS, THE GREAT STOIC PHILOSOPHER

> When a man sees his end, he would want to know that there was some purpose to his life. How will the world speak my name in the years to come? Will I be known as the philosopher? The warrior? The tyrant?[1]
>
> — *GLADIATOR*, 2000

A scene in the movie *Gladiator* (which drew liberally from Roman history) has the actor Richard Harris (playing Marcus Aurelius) contemplating on his legacy. The dialogue is fictitious, yet its substance would not have strayed far from the truth. Marcus Aurelius lived two thousand years ago, but if we wanted to know what thoughts crossed his mind, there is one document that could tell us.

The Philosophy Of Marcus Aurelius

> Remember, too, on every occasion that leads you to vexation to apply this principle: not that this is a misfortune, but that to bear it nobly is good fortune.[2]

— MARCUS AURELIUS

The *Meditations*, authored by Marcus Aurelius, is considered one of the greatest spiritual works ever written.[3] It is the only one of its kind in history and stands testament to the scope and depth of the mind of this exceptional philosopher. In it, he was giving counsel to himself, the philosopher advising the emperor, on the proper discharge of the responsibilities of his position. They are the results of the nightly self-examination that Stoicism teaches as a spiritual exercise. The following are a few of the countless insights Marcus Aurelius conveyed in the *Meditations* and stories, demonstrating their relevance in the lives of people two millennia hence.

On Our Mind: Our Greatest Asset Is Our Rational Mind

> You have power over your mind – not outside events. Realize this, and you will find strength.[4]

— MARCUS AURELIUS

Very few people do not know Stephen Hawking. His image is well known as the frail man sitting totally immobile in his wheelchair. He had no arm or hand movements, his body slumped, his head unmoving. And yet, his mind earned him the renown and respect of an entire generation.

Hawking was born in England on January 8, 1942 and studied physics at Oxford, followed by a course in cosmology in Cambridge. However, before he turned 21, Hawking was diagnosed with Lou Gehrig's disease, or amyotrophic lateral sclerosis (ALS). He was told he would live only two more years at the most, making it unlikely that he would complete his doctorate. But against all odds, Hawking attained his Ph.D. His subsequent work led to a new understanding of the universe and its earliest beginnings.[5]

As he grew older, Hawking became increasingly immobile, eventually having to use a wheelchair. By 1985, he underwent a tracheotomy that destroyed his ability to speak. For him to communicate, a speech-generating device was designed and constructed in Cambridge, powered by a software that approximated speech, that became his electronic voice. It was only by moving his cheek muscles that he was able to operate the device. Despite his limitations, he wrote books on his theories of cosmology that became bestsellers. He became a Fellow of the Royal Society, a lifetime member of the Pontifical Academy of Sciences, and a recipient of the Presidential Medal of Freedom. He was offered a knighthood but refused it because he disdained titles. He married twice, divorced twice, and had three children. He died on March 14, 2018, at the age of 76.[6]

Hawking was a man who could not physically influence anything in his external world due to his paralysis. But he used the extensive powers of his mind to influence generations to come in their views of time and space.

> I relish the rare opportunity I've been given to live the life of the mind. But I know I need my body and that it will not last forever.[7]
>
> — STEPHEN HAWKING

Marcus Aurelius constantly extolled the power of the mind above all other powers a person may possess. "The things you think about determine the quality of your mind…. Your soul takes on the color of your thoughts." Marcus Aurelius [8]

Hawking is an example of the greatness one can achieve and the difference one can make solely by using his mind. He could have become bitter and despondent, blaming his physical deformity for failing in life. Instead, he surmounted his personal obstacles and used his mind to fulfill his soul's destiny.

> If you can cut yourself – your mind – free of what other people do and say, of what you've said or done, of the things that you're afraid

will happen, the impositions of the body that contains you and the breath within, and what the whirling chaos sweeps in from outside, so that the mind is freed from fate, brought to clarity, and lives life on its own recognizance – doing what's right, accepting what happens, and speaking the truth –

If you can cut free of impressions that cling to the mind, free of the future and the past – can make yourself, as Empedocles says, 'a sphere rejoicing in its perfect stillness,' and concentrate on living what can be lived (which means the present)…then you can spend the time you have left in tranquility. And in kindness. And at peace with the spirit within you.[9]

— MARCUS AURELIUS

On Problems: We Create Problems In The Mind.

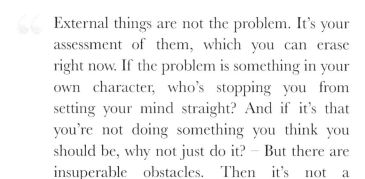

External things are not the problem. It's your assessment of them, which you can erase right now. If the problem is something in your own character, who's stopping you from setting your mind straight? And if it's that you're not doing something you think you should be, why not just do it? – But there are insuperable obstacles. Then it's not a problem. The cause of your inaction lies outside you. – But how can I go on living with that undone? Then depart, with a good conscious, as if you'd done it, embracing the obstacles too.[10]

— MARCUS AURELIUS

Winston Churchill is regarded as the Greatest Briton by the people of the United Kingdom, an honor which will likely be his for all time.[11] Churchill's greatest accomplishment was leading his country to victory in World War II as Britain's Prime Minister.

But did young Churchill also stand out among his peers the same way he did as a grown man? Although he was intelligent and had a good memory, the young Winston was unimpressive. His teachers said he was "negligent, slovenly" and always late. At 14, his housemaster said that "his forgetfulness, carelessness, unpunctuality, and irregularity in every way" earned him the lowest grades in his class. He also had a lisp and dyslexia, disabilities that affected his reading and spelling. Winston was a lonely boy, recalling, "I was, on the whole, considerably discouraged by my school days. It was not pleasant to feel … so completely outclassed and left behind." [12]

How did this troubled lad become one of the greatest leaders of the free world? Notwithstanding everything his teachers said about him, Winston had innate strengths that escaped them. He was brilliant at those things that truly interested him. When he was older, he finished at the top of his class in English and history as well as military tactics and strategy. His deep understanding of world events enabled him to clearly communicate to the British people his vision of what is necessary to win the war. When faced with dangerous situations, Winston was fearless, strong, and energetic. He developed a keen sense of human nature, and when his recurring depression beset him he turned to painting and writing for comfort. 13

According to Marcus Aurelius, our life is not a monolithic thing defined by any singular characteristic. Churchill's troublesome childhood did not set the limitations that he may achieve in his adulthood. These limitations exist only in the mind. Neither should we feel constrained by how we were characterized in the past. All these limitations and constraints are illusory and irrelevant. The challenge always is: Regardless of the past or tomorrow's possibilities, what is the best that I can do at present? That is all that matters.

 Do not disturb yourself by picturing your life as a whole; do not assemble in your mind the many and varied troubles which have come to you in the past and will come again in the future, but ask yourself with regard to every present difficulty: 'What is there in this that is unbearable and beyond endurance?' You would be ashamed to confess it! And then remind yourself that it is not the future or what has passed that afflicts you, but always the present, and the power of this is much diminished if you take it in isolation and call your mind to task if it thinks that it cannot stand up to it when taken on its own.[14]

— MARCUS AURELIUS

On How The Universe Works: The Universe Is Change

Always remember these things: what the nature of the Whole is, what my own nature is, the relation of this nature to that, what kind of part it is of what kind of Whole, and that there is no one who can prevent you keeping all that you say and do in accordance with that nature, of which you are a part.[15]

— MARCUS AURELIUS

Vincent Van Gogh is one of the best-known post-impressionist artists, but unknown to many was how unappreciated he was in his time. He was a highly emotional child, lacked self-confidence, unsure of his identity, and needed a sense of direction. In adulthood, he tried unsuccessfully to be a preacher, a bookstore clerk, and an art salesman.[16] His days were spent mostly in ill health and solitude. Then, in 1880, Van Gogh decided to be an artist. He admired the impressionism of Pisarro, Monet, and Gauguin, but had difficulty mastering this technique. He, therefore, developed his own unconventional style for which he was criticized and shunned by his peers. Legend has it that he only managed to sell one painting in his entire life; in truth, he sold two paintings and a few drawings.[17] At one time, he pursued Gauguin with a razor, but ended up cutting his ear lobe off. Suffering intermittent fits of madness, he was committed for two years in an asylum. Two months after his release in 1890, he died from a self-inflicted gunshot wound "for the good of all." [18]

At the time, Van Gogh's life seemed like an insignificant footnote in history. But today, his work is admired for its vibrant imagery, bold colors, and dramatic brushwork, the very elements he was criticized for in his time. Van Gogh paintings are now auctioned for tens of millions of dollars; his "L'homme est en mer" sold to a private collector in 2015 for $24,462,000.[19] In retrospect, Van Gogh's genius is a fixture in the universe, destined for immortality, although he was oblivious of it. He is part of the Whole, as Aurelius wrote because his tragic life that gave birth to his work has a place in human history. In retrospect, Van Gogh's struggles are linked to his immortal artwork.

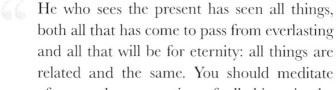

He who sees the present has seen all things, both all that has come to pass from everlasting and all that will be for eternity: all things are related and the same. You should meditate often on the connection of all things in the universe and their relationship to each other.

In a way all things are interwoven and therefore have a family feeling for each other: one thing follows another in due order through the tension of movement, the common spirit inspiring them, and the unity of all being.[20]

— MARCUS AURELIUS

Despite his madness, or maybe because of it, Van Gogh accomplished what he was destined to do in this universe during those brief ten years. His posthumous recognition as a master of modern art is an example of a person fulfilling his destiny, "doing what his nature demands," which only revealed itself nearly a century after his death.

So you were born to feel 'nice'? Instead of doing things and experiencing them? Don't you see the plants, the birds, the ants and spiders and bees going about their individual tasks, putting the world in order, as best they can? And you're not willing to do your job as a human being? Why aren't you running to do what your nature demands?[21]

— MARCUS AURELIUS

Marcus Aurelius spoke of an unfolding universe, a universe of change, and death is an inevitable part of it. Once he found his life's purpose, Van Gogh lived for the present such that even though his life was short, he left an indelible mark in this world. Imagine if he had not painted if he "died with his music still in him." The present is all we ever have at any time – not the past nor the future. We should avoid complacency and procrastination; we should fulfill our life's purpose at every waking moment.

On Happiness: You Alone Can Make Yourself Happy.

We often think the road to success should begin early in life. As children, we start school younger, race to get a slot in top universities, build a career early and get a high-paying job. It's all part of following the Great Plan we set for ourselves. Society programmed us to think this way. The first to the top is assured of success and, presumably, happiness. So, what if you were fired from a series of low-paying jobs and, at 40 years old, found yourself running a roadside gas station in rural Kentucky during the Great Depression? Far from a success story, you might say.

But Harland Sanders took life one day at a time. His service station was not earning much, so he served travelers home-cooked dinners in his own personal living quarters attached to the station. His customers happened to like his chicken, and so he spent the next ten years trying to improve it. He perfected a pressure fryer cooking method and developed a "Secret Recipe" with eleven herbs and spices that remain secret nearly a hundred years later.[22] At an age when many young people today think of retiring, Sanders opened his first restaurant across his service station and called it the Harland Sanders Café. Certainly, tough times still lay ahead, but today, the white-haired bespectacled Colonel Sanders grins at the side of every bucket of KFC chicken sold in over 24,000 outlets in more than 145 countries worldwide.

What lesson, if any, could we take away from Harland Sanders' success, which, by the way, he never planned? We could summarize it in four words: Go with the flow. Marcus Aurelius gives us some pointers.

First, do not permit the misfortunes you encounter or the actions and opinions of others, affect you negatively, even if you were fired from every job you ever had.

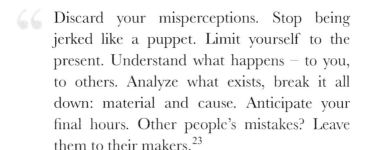

> Discard your misperceptions. Stop being jerked like a puppet. Limit yourself to the present. Understand what happens – to you, to others. Analyze what exists, break it all down: material and cause. Anticipate your final hours. Other people's mistakes? Leave them to their makers.[23]
>
> — MARCUS AURELIUS

Second, take control of how you see your environment. If you perceive your erstwhile failures as signs leading you to where you should go next, just like Sanders thought of serving his gas station guests some chicken, then explore it. The key is to accept what you cannot control but take charge of what you can control. You can choose not to be affected by something that you would ordinarily perceive to be harmful to you.

> It's all in how you perceive it. You're in control. You can dispense with misperception at will, like rounding the point. Serenity, total calm, safe anchorage. Let it happen, if it wants, to whatever it can happen to. And what's affected can complain about it if it wants. It doesn't hurt me unless I interpret its happening as harmful to me. I can choose not to.[24]

> — MARCUS AURELIUS

> Choose not to be harmed — and you won't feel harmed. Don't feel harmed — and you haven't been.[25]

> — MARCUS AURELIUS

Finally, keep reminding yourself that opportunities lie in wait if you are willing to take them.

> I was once a fortunate man but at some point fortune abandoned me. But true good fortune is what you make for yourself. Good fortune: good character, good intentions, and good actions.[26]

On Self-Improvement: Keep Progressing.

> In the morning when thou risest unwillingly, let this thought be present - I am rising to the work of a human being. Why then am I dissatisfied if I am going to do the things for which I exist and for which I was brought into the world? [27]

— MARCUS AURELIUS

Leonardo da Vinci is the genius behind the Italian Renaissance. He was a man of great talent in both science and art. However, during his day, he had a reputation as a dreamer and procrastinator who was too easily distracted. He gave the impression that he worked only a few brush strokes a day because it took him 16 years to complete the Mona Lisa, his most famous work, and 14 years to complete The Virgin of the Rocks. He sculpted and painted and constructed plans for early prototypes of planes, helicopters and submarines. He also began many projects that he never finished, but his sketches and notes turned out to be significant contributions to architecture, engineering, botany, biology, anatomy, physics and math. These did not indicate laziness but a dedication to perfection. Matteo Bandello, an Italian monk and writer, observed Leonardo as he worked on the Last Supper.

> He would arrive early, climb up onto the scaffolding, and set to work. Sometimes he stayed there from dawn to sunset, never once laying down his brush, forgetting to eat and drink, painting without pause. At other times he would go for two, three or four days without touching his brush, but spending several hours a day in front of the work, his arms folded, examining and criticizing the figures to himself. I also saw him, driven by some sudden urge, at midday, when the sun was at its height, leaving the Corte Vecchia, where he was working on his marvelous clay horse, to come straight to Santa Maria delle Crazie, without seeking shade, and clamber up on to the scaffolding, pick up a brush, put in one or two strokes, and then go away again. [28]

— MATTEO BANDELLO

Marcus Aurelius, who lived 15 centuries before Da Vinci, could very well have been describing the artist when driven, as if possessed, to achieve perfection in his work:

People who love what they do wear themselves down doing it, they even forget to wash or eat. Do you have less respect for your own nature than the engraver does for engraving, the dancer for dance, the miser for money or the social climber for status? When they're really possessed by what they do, they'd rather stop eating and sleeping than give up practicing their arts. - Marcus Aurelius [29]

Leonardo da Vinci was not a procrastinator. He was a man of many interests and skills, so he envisioned more projects than he had the opportunity to pursue. Later in life, Leonardo lamented "never having completed a single work," and pleaded with God to "Tell me if anything ever was done." [30] Leonardo may have been eccentric, but he was not a procrastinator. An example of a true procrastinator is the literary giant we shall describe next.

Victor Hugo was a writer with incredible talent and occasional bouts of listlessness. In the summer of 1829, he committed to his publisher to write The Hunchback of Notre Dame in twelve months. He spent the following year, however, on other projects and social entertainment. Twelve months elapsed and there was no book, prompting his publisher to set his new deadline at less than six months. Realizing that he needed to drastically change his work habits, Hugo stripped naked in his study. He ordered his servant to gather all his clothes and lock them up where he could not get them. Left with only a shawl to wear, Hugo was forced to stay indoors and focus on his writing. He completed Notre Dame in four months, well before the deadline. He wrote other novels, novellas, short stories, plays, and more over six decades. [31]

Think of your many years of procrastination; how the gods have repeatedly granted you further periods of grace, of which you have taken no advantage. It is time now to realise the nature of the universe to which you belong, and of that controlling Power whose offspring you are; and to understand that your time has a limit set to it. Use it, then, to advance your enlightenment; or it will be gone, and never in your power again.[32]

— MARCUS AURELIUS

Margaret Atwood is Canada's most celebrated writer. She is best known for her novel The Handmaid's Tale (1985) and its sequel The Testaments (2019). You may think that she calls herself a procrastinator (she calls herself one) because she wrote the two novels more than three decades apart. The truth is that she lived a very productive life – since 1961 she has written 14 novels, 16 volumes of poetry, 10 full-length non-fiction works, nine short story collections, and eight children's books, plus a few ebooks, librettos and television scripts. But why is she a self-confessed procrastinator? She "spends the morning procrastinating and worrying, and then plunges into the manuscript in a frenzy of anxiety around 3:00 p.m." [33] According to Atwood, "I see myself as lazy." [34] Evidently, Atwood is into the habit of putting off work, even if only by a few hours, but not out of laziness as her body of work shows. Psychologists see procrastination as more of an irregularity in mood regulation, an occasional lack of self-confidence, feeling of insecurity, stress at feeling incompetent, or fear of failure. [35]

 —But we have to sleep sometime…Agreed. But nature set a limit on that—as it did on eating and drinking. And you're over the limit. You've had more than enough of that. But not of working. There you're still below your quota. You don't love yourself enough. Or you'd love your nature too, and what it demands of you.[36]

— MARCUS AURELIUS

Marcus Aurelius' advice aligns with modern views on procrastination. "You don't love yourself enough. Or you'd love your nature, too, and what it demands of you." This statement is consistent with the feelings of inadequacy, insecurity, and lack of self-confidence that psychologists characterize procrastinators by. If talented people and those with extraordinary skills were confident in themselves, they would dive right down to work because, as Marcus says, they would love their nature and the demands it makes on them. Leonardo da Vinci, Victor Hugo, and Margaret Atwood had, through their own methods, tapped into their true nature and created masterpieces for which they are known today.

On Our Virtue: People Will Always Do Awful Things But We Are Only Responsible For Our Own Virtue.

So far in this chapter, we associated the lives of famous people to the sayings of Marcus Aurelius. In this particular segment we shall talk about one ordinary individual who could represent any one of us. Devoid of fame or fortune, he nevertheless embodies Marcus' message of being responsible for our own virtue despite whatever the external circumstances may be.

 Live out your life in truth and justice, tolerant of those who are neither true nor just. [37]

— MARCUS AURELIUS

Angel Cruz was arrested for burglary and became a juvenile delinquent at the age of 13. He was convicted for attempted murder when he was 17. Then at 22, he was convicted of armed robbery that began as a heroin sale dispute. By all indications, Angel Cruz was not a good man. Until he resolved to take control of his life and determine his own future.

 Let not future things disturb you, for you will come to them, if it shall be necessary, having with you the same reason which you now use for present things. [38]

— MARCUS AURELIUS

During his imprisonment, Angel decided to become his own legal advocate. He felt, rightly, that his prosecution had used unfair tactics that his defense failed to competently address. So, he used the prison library to study the legalities of his prosecution. "The prison library became my church," Angel said. Through his own efforts, he got the Appellate Division to toss out his case and require the trial judge to resentence. Cruz realized that there was only a slim chance that Judge Quinones would grant clemency to a twice-convicted felon. "In the end, Judge Quinones exercised grace. The judge paid my debt to the devil. After that, I belonged to God." [39]

From that time, Angel Cruz turned his life around. He went back to school, graduated from John Jay College and CUNY Law School, and served as judges' clerk. He is now married with three children, runs his own legal practice, and is a candidate for Civil Court Judge in the Bronx. He has a high sense of justice and fairness, tempering punishment with grace.

> Our actions may be impeded . . . but there can be no impeding our intentions or dispositions. Because we can accommodate and adapt. The mind adapts and converts to its own purposes the obstacle to our acting… The impediment to action advances action. What stands in the way becomes the way. [40]

> — MARCUS AURELIUS

Marcus Aurelius teaches us that we are responsible for our own virtue because our words, thoughts, and deeds are within our control. Like Angel Cruz in his youth and innocence, there are things in this world that rendered him a victim of society. But when his faculties had matured, he adapted and accommodated. Through his incarceration he developed an interest in the law and "what stood in the way became the way" – he mastered the law, and used it for his betterment. He became responsible for his own virtue.

Action Steps

There are many important lessons that Marcus Aurelius teaches us that we can convert into actionable principles in our own lives. Four of them are highly relevant to daily living.

(1) Accepting instead of resisting

 Why is it so hard when things go against you? If it's imposed by nature, accept it gladly and stop fighting it. And if not, work out what your own nature requires, and aim at that, even if it brings you no glory. None of us is forbidden to pursue our own good. [41]

— MARCUS AURELIUS

Think about what is presently your greatest obstacle – at work, in your studies, or with family relations. Does it involve other people, external situations, or things beyond your control? The first thing is to accept it. Be OK with it. Then, given these obstacles, contemplate what you can do – a change of schedule, finding a new job, compromising with another – that will minimize or resolve the problem. You will be surprised at all the possibilities once you have accepted what cannot be changed.

(2) Redirecting our mind

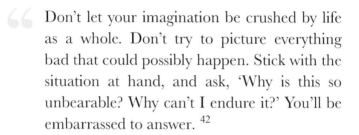

> Don't let your imagination be crushed by life as a whole. Don't try to picture everything bad that could possibly happen. Stick with the situation at hand, and ask, 'Why is this so unbearable? Why can't I endure it?' You'll be embarrassed to answer. [42]
>
> — MARCUS AURELIUS

Think of an undertaking you are currently pursuing. You may be in charge of a project at work. You may be raising school-age children, or caring for elder family members. In any undertaking, we have fears that things may go wrong, no matter how remote they may be. Contemplate a bit on these fears – what if they do happen? Then decide on a course of action. And what if they don't anyway? You would have wasted all this time uselessly worrying because there is nothing you can do about the future. Then come back to the present, and see what you can do about it NOW.

(3) Focusing on the present moment

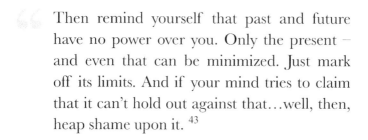

> Then remind yourself that past and future
> have no power over you. Only the present –
> and even that can be minimized. Just mark
> off its limits. And if your mind tries to claim
> that it can't hold out against that…well, then,
> heap shame upon it. [43]

— MARCUS AURELIUS

You've heard it before. "Yesterday's the past, tomorrow's
the future, but today is a gift. That's why it's called the
present." [44] Anything you do can only be done in the
present. Is there something you regret doing in the past
and wish you can go back to undo? Forget it; it's not
happening. Learn from it and move on. Is there
something you've always wanted to do but keep putting
off for another day? Write a book, learn to swim, fly the
proverbial kite? Then, this very moment, string that kite.
Sign up for that swimming class. Sit down at your table
and write the first sentence that enters your mind. There,
you've started, and don't ever stop.

(4) Exercising the agency we have

> To live a good life: We have the potential for
> it. If we can learn to be indifferent to what
> makes no difference. This is how we learn: by
> looking at each thing, both the parts and the
> whole. Keeping in mind that none of them

can dictate how we perceive it. They don't impose themselves on us. They hover before us, unmoving. It is we who generate the judgments – inscribing them on ourselves. And we don't have to. We could leave the page blank – and if a mark slips through, erase it instantly. Remember how brief is the attentiveness required. And then our lives will end. [45]

— MARCUS AURELIUS

Are there things in your life that you consider to be problems? Start with something small. "I hate how my superior gives me more work after I had done a good job." Why should it irritate you? Because he makes you work harder. Is this not a vote of confidence in your capabilities? If you saw it that way, you realize that you could be indifferent to the added struggle and instead look forward to the new challenge. You can go on to the next problem, and solve it in the same way. Exercising your agency means adopting an action or intervention to produce the best results while choosing to be indifferent to unimportant matters.

Moving On

What was Marcus Aurelius: philosopher, warrior, or tyrant? The military conquests of Rome suggest the second, stories of Christian persecutions the third. But the journey we have taken in this chapter undoubtedly shows that Marcus is first and foremost a philosopher, and only secondarily a ruler of his empire. It is because he is the first that he succeeded as the second.

Chapter Summary

- Marcus Aurelius emphasized in his teachings that our rational mind remains our greatest asset.
- He said that many of our problems are created as a matter of perception. We can only solve problems within our control, so we must distinguish them from the rest.
- The universe, according to Marcus, unfolds pursuant to its nature, and it is in our nature to accomplish the unique roles we are destined to play.
- Even if everything and everyone else around you appears to be going wrong, Marcus reminds us that we alone can make ourselves happy.
- In his Meditations, Marcus Aurelius repeatedly emphasizes that we alone are responsible for our virtue and our own self-improvement.

AFTERWORD

 Your ability to control your thoughts – treat it
with respect. It's all that protects your mind
from false perceptions – false to your nature,
and that of all rational beings. It's what makes
thoughtfulness possible, and affection for
other people, and submission to the divine. [1]

— MARCUS AURELIUS

This brief journey through the lives and teachings of
Seneca, Epictetus, and Marcus Aurelius intended to shine
a light on how we can gain better control over our lives.
While these teachings are two thousand years old, they
have as much relevance today as the day they were put
down on paper or spoken in the gardens of Rome and
Greece.

The three philosophers could not have been more
different from each other – a wealthy aristocrat, an

emancipated slave, and a reluctant emperor. In the ordinary course of events, it would be difficult to imagine how they could have the same heart and mind. But if the philosophy they lived by proved meaningful to each of them, then wouldn't such principles be useful and applicable in the lives of all people?

Seneca is called the most controversial Stoic. Many consider his life a paradox because he was wealthy and privileged although he preached the virtues of poverty and simplicity. Despite the inconsistency, Seneca showed true commitment to the Stoic principles when he dutifully carried out Nero's judgment by taking his own life. Seneca taught that our circumstances should not detract from practicing the Stoic virtues, and possessing wealth should not lead to the corruption of our resolve to live simply.

Epictetus began his philosophical studies as a slave and earned his freedom by his teachings. He gained stature for teaching that to find happiness, we should all act according to our station and within the sphere of our control. Mastery of the three disciplines of assent, action and desire will lead us to self-fulfillment, whatever social stratum we are born to. Contemplating the metaphors of life will greatly help us to envision how we can simplify and enrich our lives.

Marcus Aurelius is the reluctant emperor; sitting at the most powerful position in the world, he demonstrated an inclination towards the intellectual pursuits of a Stoic philosopher. Rather than be corrupted by the power, he faithfully discharged the burdensome duties required by his office. Through his actions as emperor, he served the people he ruled over. Through his Meditations, he became the model of a virtuous ruler for generations to come.

Three different men with three different roles and destinies. Yet they lived the same philosophy, governed by the same mind, moved by the same spirit. Today, we are benefitted by their wisdom and example, if we open our minds to the truths their writings profess. The ability to control our thoughts and use our minds are the keys to Stoicism. Mastering them will help us achieve our destiny through living a happy and virtuous life.

If you enjoyed this book, you may want to read ***Your Daily Dose Of Stoic Wisdom.***

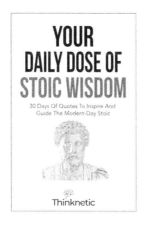

> ## Very practical way of incorporating stoicism into your daily life.
>
> I have read some other books from Thinknetic on Stoicism, I feel this book was the easiest and most well rounded book on stoicism I have read this far, not sure if it is because the other books I read, or that this book is that good. I highly recommend this book I feel everyone can get some beneficial tips to incorporate in to your life and make your days more virtuous and minimize the time you get caught up in Vise. - ★★★★★
>
> — ADAM D (AMAZON CUSTOMER)

The problem isn't that we are unhappy. It's that we expect to be happy all of the time...

Here's just a fraction of what you'll discover inside:

- The true secret to happiness and why id continues to elude so many people
- A 5-steps plan for conquering worry before it gets out of control (inspired by Marcus Aurelius' wisdom)
- Seneca's recipe to living a fuller, happier life (one "ingredient" only!)

Go to t.ly/yddosw to **get the book** or scan the code below.

Still not convinced? Go to t.ly/yddoswfc to **read a free chapter** or scan the code below.

CONTINUING YOUR JOURNEY

 Those Who Keep Learning, Will Keep Rising In Life.

— CHARLIE MUNGER (BILLIONAIRE, INVESTOR, AND WARREN BUFFET'S BUSINESS PARTNER)

The most successful people in life are those who enjoy learning and asking questions, understanding themselves and the world around them.

In our Thinknetic newsletter we'll share with you our best thinking improvement tips and tricks to help you become even more successful in life.

It's 100% free and you can unsubscribe at any time.

Besides, you'll hear first about our new releases and get the chance to receive them for free or highly discounted.

As a bonus, you'll get our bestselling book *Critical Thinking In A Nutshell* & 2 thinking improvement sheets completely for free.

Go to thinknetic.net to sign up for free!

(Or simply scan the code with your camera)

SCAN ME

REFERENCES

1. Stoicism At A Glance

1. Franklin, B. (1791) *The Autobiography of Benjamin Franklin*, [online reproduction by U.S. History.org] https://www.ushistory.org/ Franklin/autobiography/page38.htm, p.38

2. Sparks, J. (2021) "Life of Benjamin Franklin," *The Electric Ben Franklin.* U.S. History.org.https://www.ushistory.org/Franklin/ biography/app01.htm#:~:text=Franklin%20belonged.&text= BENJAMIN%20was%20the%20youngest%20son,by%20trade% 2C%20had%20preceded%20him.

3. Oxford Lexico. (2021) "Stoicism,"https://www.lexico.com/ definition/Stoicism. Accessed 26 March 2021.

4. Wiegardt, E. (2010) *The Stoic Handbook, Second Edition.* San Diego, California: Wordsmith Press.

5. Wiegardt, p.11.

6. Encyclopedia Britannica (2021) "Heraclitus: Greek Philosopher." *Britannica.* Encylophaedia Britannica, Inc. https://www.britannica. com/science/fire-combustion. Accessed 26 March 2021.

7. Gill, N.S. (2020) "What Was Plato's Famous Academy?" *ThoughtCo.* Dotdash publishing.https://www.thoughtco.com/all-about-platos-famous-academy-112520. Accessed 29 March 2021.

8. Encyclopaedia Britannica (2021) "Antisthenes, Greek philosopher." *Encyclopaedia Britannica, Inc.*https://www.britannica.com/biography/ Antisthenes

9. Encyclopaedia Britannica (2021) "Diogenes, Greek philosopher." *Encyclopaedia Britannica, Inc.*https://www.britannica.com/biography/ Diogenes-Greek-philosopher

10. Wiegart, p.12

11. Encyclopaedia Britannica (2021) "Crates of Thebes, Greek philosopher." *Encyclopaedia Britannica, Inc.*https://www.britannica. com/biography/Crates-of-Thebes

12. "Stoicism" (2021) *Internet Encyclopedia of Philosophy.*https://iep.utm. edu/stoicism/#H3. Accessed May 5, 2021

13. McAvoy, M. (2016) "Zeno of Citium's Philosophy of Stoicism," *A With Honors Projects*, 170,http://spark.parkland.edu/ah/170, p. 1.

14. Mark, J.J. (2014) "The Life and Thought of Zeno of Citium in Diogenes Laertius." *World History Encyclopedia.* https://www.ancient.eu/article/741/the-life-and-thought-of-zeno-of-citium-in-diogenes/. Accessed 30 March 2021.

15. Mark, par. 2. Quote attributed to Prof. Forrest E. Baird.

16. Stephens, W.O. (2021) "Musonius Rufus," *Internet Encyclopedia of Philosophy.* https://iep.utm.edu/musonius/#:https://iep.utm.edu/musonius/#:~:text=Gaius%20Musonius%20Rufus%20was%20one,%2C%20Epictetus%2C%20and%20Marcus%20Aurelius.&text=He%20affirmed%20Stoic%20orthodoxy%20in,none%20of%20them%20are%20evils. Accessed 30 March 2021.

17. Stephens, par. 3

18. Stephens, par. 20

19. Stephens, par. 22

20. Wagoner, R. (2021) "Lucius Annaeus Seneca (c. 4 B.C.E. – 65 C.E.)" *Internet Encyclopedia of Philosophy, A Peer-Reviewed Academic Resource.* https://iep.utm.edu/seneca/#:https://iep.utm.edu/seneca/#:~:text=The%20ancient%20Roman%20philosopher%20Seneca,been%20widely%20read%20Stoic%20texts.&text=Seneca%20also%20writes%20to%20criticize,values%20of%20his%20fellow%20Romans. Accessed 31 March 2021.

21. "Comparing and Contrasting the Stoicism of Seneca, Epictetus, and Marcus Aurelius." (2016) *The Education of a Millennial.*https://educationofamillennial.wordpress.com/2016/03/07/comparing-and-contrasting-the-stoicism-of-seneca-epictetus-and-marcus-aurelius/. (Accessed 1 April 2021). Par. 5.

22. Medrut, F. (2019) "30 Seneca Quotes to Help You Live a Fulfilling and Worthwhile Life." *Goalcast.* https://www.goalcast.com/2019/03/15/seneca-quotes/. Accessed 1 April 2021. Par. 8

23. Medrut, (2019) par. 10

24. Medrut, (2019) par. 31

25. Seddon, K.H. (2021) "Epictetus (55-135 C.E.)" *Internet Encyclopedia of Philosophy, A Peer-Reviewed Academic Resource.* https://iep.utm.edu/epictetu/#:~:text=Epictetus%20(55%E2%80%93135%20C.E.),Citium%20was%20established%20in%20Athens. Accessed 31 March 2021.

26. Pigliucci, M. (2017) *How to Be a Stoic: Using Ancient Philosophy to Live a Modern Life.* Basic Books; Fideler, D. (2021) "About Stoicism: A Brief Introduction." *Stoic Insight.* https://www.stoicinsights.com/about-stoicism/. Accessed 1 April 2021, par. 16.

27. "100 Great Quotes by Epictetus, the Author of the Art of Living." (2021) *The Famous People.* https://quotes.thefamouspeople.com/epictetus-1350.php. Accessed 1 April 2021, par. 12

28. *The Famous People*, p.14
29. *The Famous People*, p.17
30. Sellars, J. (2021) "Marcus Aurelius (121-180 C.E.)" *Internet Encyclopedia of Philosophy, A Peer-Reviewed Academic Resource.* https://iep.utm.edu/marcus/. Accessed 31 March 2021.
31. *The Education of a Millennial*, par.6
32. Medrut, F. (2018) "The Best of Marcus Aurelius Quotes About Life, Death, Stoicism and Leadership." *Goalcast.* https://www.goalcast.com/2018/05/11/20-marcus-aurelius-quotes/. Accessed 1 April 2021. Par. 6
33. Medrut (2018), par.8.
34. Medrut (2018), par.13.
35. The Daily Stoic (2021) "What is Stoicism? A Definition & 9 Stoic Exercises to Get You Started." *Daily Stoic: Ancient Wisdom for Everyday Life.* https://dailystoic.com/what-is-stoicism-a-definition-3-stoic-exercises-to-get-you-started// Accessed 10 April 2021.
36. Magee, Z. (2009, December 23) "Prince William Sleeps on the Streets with Homeless." *ABC News.* https://abcnews.go.com/International/prince-william-sleeps-streets/story?id=9401023. Accessed 10 April 2021.
37. Robertson, D.J. (2020, Feb. 4) "The Stoicism of Benjamin Franklin." *Medium.* https://medium.com/stoicism-philosophy-as-a-way-of-life/the-stoicism-of-benjamin-franklin-21ed64abb4ab.

2. Seneca The Younger – The Most Controversial Stoic

1. Philo-Notes (2021) "Seneca Quotes." *Philo-Notes.* https://philonotes.com/index.php/2020/10/08/seneca-quotes/. Accessed 10 April, 2021.
2. Daily Stoic (2021) "Humility Kills Pride." *Daily Stoic.* https://dailystoic.com/humility-kills-pride/. Accessed 10 April 2021.
3. Inwood, B. (1995) Seneca in His Philosophical Milieu, *Harvard Studies in Classical Philology*, 97, 63-76. doi:10.2307/311301, p.7
4. Inwood, p. 69
5. Di Paola, O. (2014) Philosophical thought of the School of the Sextii. *Epeikena International Journal of Ontology History and Critics.* 4(1-2): 327-339
6. Wilson, E.R. (2014) *The Greatest Empire: A Life of Seneca*, Oxford University Press, p. 56

7. Seneca, *Moral letters to Lucilius (Letter 108)* Epistles CVIII On the Approaches to Philosophy, 20-21

8. Natur. Quaest. iii. 27

9. Wasson, D.L. (2013) "Quaestor," *World History Encyclopedia.* Ancient History Encyclopedia Ltd. https://www.worldhistory.org/Quaestor/. Accessed April 7, 2021

10. "Seneca: On Providence." (2016) *How to Be a Stoic.* https://howtobeastoic.wordpress.com/2016/11/17/seneca-on-providence/. Accessed April 7, 2021.

11. Motto, A.L. (1966) Seneca on Trial: The Case of the Opulent Stoic. *The Classical Journal*, 61(6): 354-358

12. Encyclopedia Britannica (2021) "Caligula: Roman Emperor." *Britannica.* Encyclopedia Britannica, Inc. https://www.britannica.com/biography/Caligula-Roman-emperor. Accessed April 7, 2021.

13. Erenow (2021) "Death for Burrus and Octavia," *Ancient History and Civilization.* Erenow, p.19. *https://erenow.net/ancient/blood-of-the-caesars-how-the-murder-of-germanicus-led-to-the-fall-of-rome/19.php*

14. Erenow, p. 19

15. Wilson, (2014), p. 123

16. Motto (1966), p. 254

17. Motto (1966), p. 254

18. Farrar, F.W. (1874) *Seekers after God.* Project Gutenberg, Pp. 53-54

19. Motto (1966), p. 255

20. Wilson, E. (2014) *The Greatest Empire: A Life of Seneca.* New York, NY: Oxford University Press, p. 131.

21. Motto (1966), p. 255

22. Wilson, (2014), p.201

23. Wilson (2014), p. 201

24. Wilson (2014), p. 201

25. Seneca, "On the Shortness of Life," 7.3

26. Wilson (2014), p. 208

27. Medrut, F. (2019) "30 Seneca Quotes to Help You Live a Fulfilling and Worthwhile Life." *Goalcast.* https://www.goalcast.com/2019/03/15/seneca-quotes/. Accessed 1 April 2021. Par. 8

28. Medrut, (2019) par. 10

29. Medrut, (2019) par. 31

30. Ferguson, C. (2015) "Throw Me to the Wolves & I'll Return Leading the Pack." *LeadChange.* https://leadchangegroup.com/throw-me-to-the-wolves-and-ill-return-leading-the-pack/. Accessed April 10, 2021

3. Seneca's Essays And Letters That Are Grounded On Stoicism

1. Hughes, A.J. (2017) "Letters from a Stoic – Seneca." *Alex. J. Hughes.* https://www.alexjhughes.com/books/2017/2/13/letters-from-a-stoic-seneca. Accessed 10 April 2021

2. Grauschopf, S. (2020) "Lottery Curse Victims: 7 People Who Won Big & Lost Everything." *The Balance Everyday.* https://www.thebalanceeveryday.com/lottery-curse-victims-896653. Accessed 10 April 2021

3. Wilson (2014) p. 229

4. Wilson (2014), p. 229

5. Wilson (2014), p. 236

6. Wilson (2014), p. 243

7. Stock, G.W.J, (2014) *A Guide to Stoicism.* Project Gutenberg, location 265

8. Daily Stoic (2021) "Never Be a Slave of Your Wealth." *Daily Stoic.* https://dailystoic.com/never-slave-to-wealth/#:~:text=%E2%80%9CFor%20the%20wise%20man%20does,him%20to%20practice%20his%20virtue.%E2%80%9D. Accessed April 10, 2021

9. Munk, N. (2016) "How Warren Buffett's Son Would Feed the World." *The Atlantic.* https://www.theatlantic.com/magazine/archive/2016/05/how-warren-buffetts-son-would-feed-the-world/476385/. Accessed April 15, 2021

10. Elkins, K. (2016) "Billionaires Warren Buffett and Bill Gates have similar ideas about how much money you should leave your kids." *Make It.* CNBC. https://www.cnbc.com/2016/09/26/warren-buffett-bill-gates-have-similar-ideas-on-how-much-money-to-leave-kids.html. Accessed April 12, 2021.

11. Daily Stoic (2021) "Never Be a Slave of Your Wealth." *Daily Stoic.* https://dailystoic.com/never-slave-to-wealth/. Accessed April 15, 2021.

12. Seneca, L.A. (2010) *Selected Letters.* Oxford University Press, p. 91

13. Cohen, K. (2020) "The rise and fall of Lance Armstrong: What you need to know before watching 'LANCE'." *ESPN.* https://www.espn.com/olympics/story/_/id/29177242/the-rise-fall-lance-armstrong-need-know-watching-lance. Accessed April 15, 2021.

14. Cohen (2020).

15. Edwards (1997) p. 27

16. Edwards, C. (1997) Self-Scrutiny and Self-Transformation in Seneca's Letters. *Greece & Rome*, 44 (1): 23-38, p. 30

17. Edwards (1997) p. 30
18. Fairfield (n.d.) "**XXVIII** On Travel as a Cure for Discontent." http://faculty.fairfield.edu/rosivach/cl104/seneca.htm. Accessed April 15, 2021.
19. Edwards (1997) p. 30
20. How to be a Stoic (2021) "Seneca on Anger, Part I," *How to be a Stoic*. https://howtobeastoic.wordpress.com/2017/02/09/seneca-on-anger-part-i/. Accessed April 10, 2021
21. Gambardella, S. (2019) "Seneca: Curbing Anger." *The Sophist*. https://medium.com/the-sophist/seneca-curbing-anger-cde88b588d5d. Accessed April 15, 2021
22. How to be a Stoic (2021) "Seneca on Anger, Part I," *How to be a Stoic*. https://howtobeastoic.wordpress.com/2017/02/09/seneca-on-anger-part-i/. Accessed April 10, 2021
23. Seneca the Younger (1925) *The Tao of Seneca* Vol. 3: Based on the Moral Letters to Lucilius. Translated by Richard Mott Gummere. Loeb Classical Library, p. 196
24. Seneca the Younger (1925) *The Tao of Seneca* Vol. 3: Based on the Moral Letters to Lucilius. Translated by Richard Mott Gummere. Loeb Classical Library, p. 197
25. Jasuja, M. (2019) "From Brat to Champion: Roger Federer's Story of Mental Transformation." *Linked-In Pulse*. https://www.linkedin.com/pulse/from-brat-champion-roger-federers-story-mental-monica-jasuja/. Accessed April 15, 2021.
26. Jasuja (2019)
27. Seneca (1969) Letters from a Stoic. Translated by Robin Campbell. Penguin Books, Inc., p.7
28. Vocabulary.com (2021) "Grandiloquence." *Vocabulary.com*. https://www.vocabulary.com/dictionary/grandiloquence#:https://www.vocabulary.com/dictionary/grandiloquence#:~:text=Grandiloquence%20is%20a%20lofty%2C%20high,fluff%20but%20may%20lack%20substance.&text=Grandiloquence%20comes%20from%20the%20Latin,and%20other%20words%20about%20talk. Accessed April 15, 2021
29. Liptak, A. (2016) "Clarence Thomas Breaks 10 Years of Silence at Supreme Court." *The New York Times*. https://www.nytimes.com/2016/03/01/us/politics/supreme-court-clarence-thomas.html. Accessed April 15, 2021.
30. Seneca the Younger (1917) *The Tao of Seneca Vol. 1: Based on the Moral Letters to Lucilius.* Translated by Richard Mott Gummere. Loeb Classical Library, p. 285
31. Popova, M. (2021) "The Shortness of Life: Seneca on the Busyness and the Art of Living Wide Rather than Living Long." *Brain

Pickings. https://www.brainpickings.org/2014/09/01/seneca-on-the-shortness-of-life/

32. Daily Stoic (2021) "Letters from a Stoic by Seneca: Book Summary, Key Lessons and Best Quotes." *Daily Stoic.* https://dailystoic.com/letters-from-a-stoic/. Accessed April 10, 2021

33. Seneca the Younger (1917) The Tao of Seneca Vol. 1: Based on the Moral Letters to Lucilius. Translated by Richard Mott Gummere. Loeb Classical Library, p. 103

34. "Idiomatic Expressions" (2021) *My English Pages.com.* https://www.myenglishpages.com/english/random-idiom.php?c=767. Accessed April 15, 2021. Note, the second line was added by anonymous authors subsequently.

35. Chandler, T. (2012) "Seneca on Leisure", *Colloquy Text Theory Critique*, 23(2012): 214-222. Mpnash University., p. 217-218

36. Chandler (2012) p. 220

37. Chandler (2012) p. 221

38. Seneca the Younger (1917) *The Tao of Seneca Vol. 1: Based on the Moral Letters to Lucilius.* Translated by Richard Mott Gummere. Loeb Classical Library, p. 286

39. Nagesh, A. (2015) "Nepal is banning disabled climbers from Everest, so here are seven people that totally nailed it." *Metro.* https://metro.co.uk/2015/09/29/nepal-is-banning-disabled-climbers-from-everest-so-here-are-seven-people-that-totally-nailed-it-5413581/. Accessed 15 April 2021

40. Daily Stoic (2021) "How To Say 'No': Advice From The World's Most Powerful Man." *Daily Stoic.* https://dailystoic.com/how-to-say-no-advice-from-the-worlds-most-powerful-man/. Accessed April 15, 2021

41. Inventionland (2021) "Ten Kid Inventors Who Changed Our Lives." *Inventionland.* https://inventionland.com/blog/ten-kid-inventors-that-changed-our-lives/. Accessed April 15, 2021

42. Seneca the Younger (1920) *The Tao of Seneca Vol. 2: Based on the Moral Letters to Lucilius.* Translated by Richard Mott Gummere. Loeb Classical Library, p. 279

43. Seneca the Younger (1920) *The Tao of Seneca Vol. 2: Based on the Moral Letters to Lucilius.* Translated by Richard Mott Gummere. Loeb Classical Library, p. 280

44. Seneca, L.A. (n.d.) "On the Quality, as Contrasted with the Length, of Life, Letter XCIII." https://trisagionseraph.tripod.com/Texts/Letters/Letter93.html. Accessed April 15, 2021.

45. Seneca the Younger (1917) The Tao of Seneca Vol. 1: Based on the Moral Letters to Lucilius. Translated by Richard Mott Gummere. Loeb Classical Library, p. 83

46. Seneca the Younger (1917) The Tao of Seneca Vol. 1: Based on the Moral Letters to Lucilius. Translated by Richard Mott Gummere. Loeb Classical Library, p. 116
47. Seneca the Younger (1920) The Tao of Seneca Vol. 2: Based on the Moral Letters to Lucilius. Translated by Richard Mott Gummere. Loeb Classical Library, pp. 52-53.

4. Epictetus – A Slave Becoming The Most Sought-After Stoic Philosopher

1. Farrar, F.W. (2004) *Seekers After God*. Project Gutenberg, eBook #10846, loc. 2147
2. Seddon, K.H. (2021) "Epictetus (55-135 C.E.)" *Internet Encyclopedia of Philosophy, A Peer-Reviewed Academic Resource.* https://iep.utm.edu/epictetu/#:~:text=Epictetus%20(55%E2%80%93135%20C.E.),Citium%20was%20established%20in%20Athens. Accessed March 31, 2021.
3. Encyclopaedia Britannica (2021) Epictetus, Greek Philosopher. *Britannica.* https://www.britannica.com/biography/Epictetus-Greek-philosopher. Accessed April 15 2021.
4. Encyclopaedia Britannica (2021) Epictetus, Greek Philosopher. *Britannica.* https://www.britannica.com/biography/Epictetus-Greek-philosopher. Accessed April 15 2021.
5. Oldfather, W.A. (1956) *Epictetus, The Discourses as Reported by Arrian, the Manual, and Fragments.* Harvard University Press, Cambridge, Massachusetts, p.viii
6. Oldfather, (1956), p. vii
7. Epictetus, Discourses, i.7.32, http://classics.mit.edu/Epictetus/discourses.html. Accessed April 15, 2021
8. Origen, Contra Celcus. Book VII, Chapter LIII. http://www.earlychristianwritings.com/text/origen167.html. Accessed April 15, 2021.
9. Long, A.A. (2002) *Epictetus: A Stoic and Socratic Guide to Life.* Department of Classics, University of California, Berkeley, ISBN 0199245568, p. 10
10. Origen, Contra Celcus. Book VII, Chapter LIII. http://www.earlychristianwritings.com/text/origen167.html. Accessed April 15, 2021.
11. Simplicius, *Commentary on the Enchiridion*, XIII
12. Encyclopedia Britannica (2021)

13. The Suda (i.e., Stronghold) refers to a massive 10th-century Byzantine Greek encyclopedia that contained more than 31,000 entries drawn from sources that have since been lost. (History of information, https://www.historyofinformation.com/detail.php?id=2502)

14. Internet Encyclopedia of Philosophy (2021) Epictetus (55-135 C.E.). https://iep.utm.edu/epictetu/#H3. Accessed April 15, 2021.

15. History of the Christian Church. (n.d.) 91. Epictetus. https://www.ccel.org/ccel/schaff/hcc2.v.x.iv.html. Accessed April 15, 2021.

16. Simplicius, *Commentary on the Enchiridion*, XLVI.

17. Investopedia (2020, March 25) "Which Consumer Goods Do Americans Buy the Most?" *Investopedia.* https://www.investopedia.com/ask/answers/051215/which-consumer-goods-do-americans-buy-most.asp. Accessed April 20, 2021

5. Epictetus' Discourses And Handbook: His Take On Stoicism

1. Cadena, R. (2020) "Epictetus: A Brief Biography of the Slave, Stoic Philosopher." *Rick Cadena.* https://rickycadena99.medium.com/epictetus-a-brief-biography-of-the-slave-stoic-philosopher-d7753cca0372. Accessed April 18, 2021.

2. Whelan, E (2019) "Epictetus: Philosophy as a Guide to Life." *Classical Wisdom.* https://classicalwisdom.com/. Accessed April 16, 2021

3. Mark, J.J. (2011) "Epictetus." *World History Encyclopedia.* https://www.worldhistory.org/Epictetus/#:~:text=According%20to%20Epictetus%2C%20the%20logos,the%20universe%20by%20immutable%20laws. Accessed April 16, 2021

4. Mark (2011), par. 11

5. History.com (2021) "Joan of Arc is burned at the stake for heresy." *History.* https://www.history.com/this-day-in-history/joan-of-arc-martyred. Accessed April 16, 2021

6. "Epictetus" (2021) *Internet Encyclopedia of Philosophy.* https://iep.utm.edu/epictetu/#SH4c. Accessed April 16, 2021.

7. Hard, Robin (1995) The Discourses of Epictetus. ed. with introduction and notes by Christopher Gill. London: Everyman/Dent. Reproduced in "Epictetus," *Internet Encyclopedia of Philosophy.* https://iep.utm.edu/epictetu/#SH4c. Accessed April 16, 2021

8. Long, George (1890) *The Discourses of Epictetus with the Encheiridion and Fragments*. London: George Bell. First published 1848.

9. "Epictetus" (2021) *Internet Encyclopedia of Philosophy*. https://iep.utm. edu/epictetu/#SH4c. Accessed April 16, 2021

10. Matheson, P. E. (1916). *Epictetus: The Discourses and Manual*. 2 vols. Oxford: Clarendon Press. Reproduced in "Epictetus" *Internet Encyclopedia of Philosophy*. https://iep.utm.edu/epictetu/#SH4c. Accessed April 16, 2021.

11. Hard (1995), reproduced in *Internet Encyclopedia of Philosophy*.

12. Oldfather, W.A. (1956) *Epictetus, The Discourses as Reported by Arrian, the Manual, and Fragments*. Harvard University Press, Cambridge, Massachusetts

13. Sadler, G. (2020) "Stoic Inner Citadels by Greg Sadler." *Modern Stoicism*. https://modernstoicism.com/stoic-inner-citadels-by-greg-sadler/. Accessed April 16, 2021.

14. Sadler, (2020)

15. "Epictetus (55-135 C.E.)" (2021) *Internet Encyclopedia of Philosophy*. https://iep.utm.edu/epictetu/#SH4c. Accessed April 16, 2021.

16. Daily Stoic (2021) "Enchiridion (Epictetus): Book Summary, Key Lessons and Best Quotes." *Daily Stoic: Ancient Wisdom for Everyday Life*. https://dailystoic.com/enchiridion-epictetus/#:~:text=For%20the%20Stoics%2C%20character%E2%80%94and,approve%20of%0a%20virtuous%20action. Accessed April 16, 2021.

17. "Sec. 91. Epictetus" (2021) *History of the Christian Church*. Christian Classics Ethereal Library. https://www.ccel.org/ccel/schaff/hcc2.v.x.iv.html. Accessed April 20, 2021

18. "Epictetus (55-135 C.E.)" (2021) *Internet Encyclopedia of Philosophy*. https://iep.utm.edu/epictetu/#SH4c. Accessed April 16, 2021.

19. Epictetus, (1904) *Discourses of Epictetus*, translated by George Long. D. Appleton and Company, New York, p. 105.

20. Epictetus, (1904) *Discourses of Epictetus*, translated by George Long. D. Appleton and Company, New York, p. 105.

21. Tremblay, M. (2016) Spiritual Exercises in Epictetus: Difficult but Justified. Masters thesis in Philosophy, Carleton University, Ottawa, Ontario

22. Tremblay (2016), p. 85

6. Marcus Aurelius – The Reluctant And The Last Good Emperor

1. Fabrega, Marelisa (2021) "7 Lessons on Life and Happiness from a Stoic. (Marcus Aurelius)" *Daring to Live Fully.* https://daringtolivefully.com/marcus-aurelius-quotes Accessed May 5, 2021.
2. "The Charge of the Light Brigade, by Alfred, Lord Tennyson" (2017) *Poetry Foundation.* https://www.poetryfoundation.org/poems/45319/the-charge-of-the-light-brigade. Accessed May 5, 2021.
3. Farrar, F.W. (2004) *Seekers After God.* Project Gutenberg., p. 2967
4. Vermeulen, Marian (2020) "Marcus Aurelius Part II: Triumph and Tragedy." *Time Travel Rome.* https://www.timetravelrome.com/2020/01/06/marcus-aurelius-part-ii-triumph-and-tragedy/. Accessed May 10, 2921.
5. Edward Gibbon, author of "The History of the Decline and Fall of the Roman Empire," as quoted in Fabrega (2021), par. 2.
6. "Marcus Aurelius Part III: From Gold to Rust and Iron." (2020) *Time Travel Rome.* https://www.timetravelrome.com/2020/02/27/marcus-aurelius-from-gold-to-rust-and-iron/. Accessed May 10, 2021
7. Sedgwick, Henry Dwight. (2016) *Marcus Aurelius*, Forgotten Books.com . FB&c Ltd., p. 30
8. Marcus Aurelius, *Meditations*, Book XI, 1, in Sedgwick (2016)
9. Marcus Aurelius, *Meditations*, Book IX, 42, in Sedgwick (2016)
10. Vermeulen, Marian. (2020) "Marcus Aurelius Part II: Triumph and Tragedy." *Time Travel Rome.* https://www.timetravelrome.com/2020/01/06/marcus-aurelius-part-ii-triumph-and-tragedy/. Accessed May 10, 2021.
11. Foxe, John (2010) The Fourth Persecution, Under Marcus Aurelius Antoninus, A.D. 162. *Foxe's Book of Martyrs: A history of the lives, sufferings, and triumphant deaths of the early Christians and the Protestant martyrs.* Expanded Edition. Amazon Kindle.
12. Keresztes, Paul (2011) "Marcus Aurelius a Persecutor?" *Cambridge Core.* Cambridge University Press. https://www.cambridge.org/core/journals/harvard-theological-review/article/abs/marcus-aurelius-a-persecutor/E8F76CB327530CF310251FDFCC1ADDF2 Accessed May 15, 2021.
13. Robertson, Donald. (2017) "Did Marcus Aurelius Persecute the Christians?" *Donald Robertson.* https://donaldrobertson.-

name/2017/01/13/did-marcus-aurelius-persecute-the-christians/. Accessed May 15, 2021.

14. Irenacus, Against Heresies, translated by Alexander Roberts and William Rambaut, Book IV, Chapter 30, section 3

15. Robertson, Donald. (2018) "The Death of Marcus Aurelius," *Donald Robertson: How to Think Like a Roman Emperor.* https://donaldrobertson.name/2018/01/25/the-death-of-marcus-aurelius/. Accessed May 15, 2021.

16. Robertson (2018)

17. Marcus Aurelius, *Meditations*, Book Vii,15, in Sedgwick (2016)

7. The Meditations Of Marcus Aurelius, The Great Stoic Philosopher

1. Wick, Douglas, Franzoni, David, Lustig, Branko (Producers) & Ridley Scott(Director) (2000) *Gladiator.* [Motion picture]. United States: Scott Free Productions and Red Wagon Entertainment

2. Vermuelen, Marian (2020) "Marcus Aurelius Part II: Triumph and Tragedy." *Time Travel: Ancient Rome.* https://www.timetravelrome.com/2020/01/06/marcus-aurelius-part-ii-triumph-and-tragedy/ Accessed May 5, 2021

3. Rose, Katharine. (2019) "Marcus Aurelius on How to Control the Mind." Thrive Global. https://thriveglobal.com/stories/how-to-control-the-mind-according-to-marcus-aurelius-meditations/. Accessed Mat 23, 2021.

4. Warrilow, Stephen. (2021) "Marcus Aurelius" *Zen Tools for Tough Times.* https://www.zen-tools.net/marcus-aurelius.html. Accessed May 10, 2021.

5. Redd, Nola Taylor (2019) "Stephen Hawking Biography (1942-2018)." *Space.com.* https://www.space.com/15923-stephen-hawking.html. Accessed May 23, 2021

6. Redd, Nola Taylor (2019) "Stephen Hawking Biography (1942-2018)." *Space.com.* https://www.space.com/15923-stephen-hawking.html. Accessed May 23, 2021

7. Redd, Nola Taylor (2019) "Stephen Hawking Biography (1942-2018)." *Space.com.* https://www.space.com/15923-stephen-hawking.html. Accessed May 23, 2021

8. Rose (2019)

9. Rose (2019)

10. Rose (2019)

11. Watt, Anne (2015) "Overcoming Obstacles: How Winston Churchill's Struggles Fueled Success." *K12: Learning Liftoff*. https://www.learningliftoff.com/overcoming-obstacles-winston-churchill/. Accessed May 23, 2021

12. Watt (2015)

13. Watt (2015)

14. Good Reads (2021) "Marcus Aurelius, Quotes" *Good Reads*. https://www.goodreads.com/author/quotes/17212.Marcus_Aurelius?page=4. Accessed May 10, 2021

15. Warrilow, Stephen. (2021) "Marcus Aurelius" *Zen Tools for Tough Times. https://www.zen-tools.net/marcus-aurelius.html.* May 10, 2021.

16. The Van Gogh Gallery (2021) "Vincent Van Gogh Biography." *The Van Gogh Gallery.* https://www.vangoghgallery.com/misc/biography.html. Accessed May 23, 2021

17. Dorsey, John (1998) "The van Gogh legend — a different picture. The story that the artist sold just one painting in his lifetime endures. In fact, he sold at least two." *The Baltimore Sun.* https://www.baltimoresun.com/news/bs-xpm-1998-10-25-1998298006-story.html. Accessed May 23, 2021.

18. The Van Gogh Gallery (2021) "Vincent Van Gogh Biography." *The Van Gogh Gallery.* https://www.vangoghgallery.com/misc/biography.html. Accessed May 23, 2021.

19. Lin, Amy (2019) "The Most Expensive Van Gogh Paintings Sold in the Auction Room." *Widewalls.* https://www.widewalls.ch/magazine/most-expensive-van-gogh-paintings-auction. Accessed May 23, 2021.

20. Warrilow (2021)

21. Good Reads (2021)

22. Scottberg, Erin (2021) "9 Famous People Who Will Inspire You to Never Give Up." *The Muse. https://www.themuse.com/advice/9-famous-people-who-will-inspire-you-to-never-give-up.* Accessed May 23, 2021.

23. Rose (2019)

24. Rose (2019)

25. Warrilow (2021)

26. Good Reads (2021)

27. Good Reads (2021)

28. Currey, Mason (2020, March 30) "Was Leonardo da Vinci a procrastinator?" *Subtle Maneuvers.* https://subtlemaneuvers.substack.com/p/was-leonardo-da-vinci-a-procrastinator#:~:text=Leonardo%20da%20Vinci%20(1452%E2%80%931519)&text=Leonardo%20did%20leave%20many%20projects,him%20three%20years%20to%20complete.. Accessed May 25, 2021

29. Good Reads (2021)

30. "Famous Procrastinators." (n.d.) *Procrastination and Science*. https://procrastinus.com/procrastination/famous-procrastinators/. Accessed May 25, 2021.

31. Clear, James. (2016, October 3) "What Victor Hugo can teach us about procrastination." *The Week*. https://theweek.com/articles/647298/what-victor-hugo-teach-about-procrastination. Accessed May 25, 2021.

32. Good Reads (2021)

33. "Famous Procrastinators." (n.d.) *Procrastination and Science*. https://procrastinus.com/procrastination/famous-procrastinators/. Accessed May 25, 2021.

34. Chen, Daryl. (2020, Mar. 12) "This is the real reason you procrastinate – and how to break the habit." *We Humans*. https://ideas.ted.com/this-is-the-real-reason-you-procrastinate-and-how-to-break-the-habit/#:~:text=In%20fact%2C%20revered%20author%20Margaret,isn't%20one%20of%20them. Accessed May 25, 2021.

35. Chen, (2020).

36. Good Reads (2021)

37. Good Reads (2021)

38. Warrilow (2021)

39. Marlee, Sierra. (2021, May 31). "Ex-con spent over 10 years in prison is now running for Judge in the Bronx." *BPR Business and Politics*. https://www.bizpacreview.com/2021/05/31/ex-con-spent-over-10-years-in-prison-is-now-running-for-judge-in-the-bronx-1082020/?utm_medium=Newsletter&utm_source=Get+Response&utm_term=EMAIL&utm_content=Newsletter&utm_campaign=bizpac. Accessed June 1, 2021.

40. Warrilow (2021)

41. Rose (2019)

42. Rose (2019)

43. Rose (2019)

44. "Bil Keane Quotes." (n.d.) *Brainy Quote.com*. https://www.brainyquote.com/quotes/bil_keane_121860. Accessed June 1, 2021

45. Rose (2019)

Afterword

1. Rose (2019)

DISCLAIMER

The information contained in this book and its components, is meant to serve as a comprehensive collection of strategies that the author of this book has done research about. Summaries, strategies, tips and tricks are only recommendations by the author, and reading this book will not guarantee that one's results will exactly mirror the author's results.

The author of this book has made all reasonable efforts to provide current and accurate information for the readers of this book. The author and its associates will not be held liable for any unintentional errors or omissions that may be found.

The material in the book may include information by third parties. Third party materials comprise of opinions expressed by their owners. As such, the author of this book does not assume responsibility or liability for any third party material or opinions.

Printed in Great Britain
by Amazon